I Am Sarah Femme

Kasey Matthews Johnson

Fulton Books
Meadville, PA

Published by Fulton Books 2024

ISBN 979-8-89221-875-7 (paperback)
ISBN 979-8-89427-704-2 (hardcover)
ISBN 979-8-89221-876-4 (digital)

Logo/Title design by Heins Creative, Inc. (Jim Heins)

Printed in the United States of America

For my husband, strength comes in many forms.
You are the strongest man I've ever met.
For my children, all three of them.
For my best friend Trina, you are my soul sister and "my person."
I love you.

I Am Sarah Femme

Kasey Matthews Johnson

I've tried to start this book about a thousand times now. This book is not going to go the way you think it's going to go. Isn't that life, though?

What once started as a memoir of whining and complaints and stories no one really cared about, was hijacked.

My memoir was commandeered by Sarah, Sarah Femme For Short.

How It All Started

Right off the bat, I'll tell you that my mind thinks in music and my mind thinks in movie lines. I am going to refer to some movie titles and song titles in this book. These are all movies (and actors) that I really enjoyed and have stuck with me over the years.

I encourage you all to take another look at these movies and any song titles and artists' names I mention here. Take a look and listen with new eyes and ears when you're finished.

If you get out of this book what Sarah wants you to get out of it, you may be a changed person.

I don't really watch many movies these days but I've seen enough to write this book using them. So "Effie…brace yourself" (*Mrs. Doubtfire*). Too long ago? Oh well.

Doesn't everyone think in movie lines?

"Bueller…Bueller" (*Ferris Bueller's Day Off*).

Also, I should warn you. I'm not a BS kind of person. I am usually pretty serious and reserved but mostly to people who just don't know or understand who I am.

I typically don't care for small talk. I long for substance.

I tell it like it is, and I'm very direct.

I try to never hurt anyone intentionally, and I am a genuine person.

I don't care for people who are two-faced, and I can spot them a mile away.

I am very introverted and enjoy spending time alone, probably more than the average person.

I am a wife and lover, sister, friend, daughter, granddaughter, aunt, cousin, and most importantly, a mom.

M-O-M.

I'm saying it louder for all those people in the back.

And to all the MOMs who've ever lost a baby, I hear you. I am you.

I am going to shout this one from the rooftops because I once had a man at work in the year 2010/2011 tell me that I shouldn't celebrate to others in the workplace that I was a "mom."

He felt it looked weak in a male-dominated field and that others wouldn't take me seriously.

He said he thought they'd always look at me as "just" being a mom.

Well, here's a news flash.

I guess I just don't care if other people think being a mom looks weak.

I guess that I also have a pretty good memory too.

(That man knows who he is, and I just want to say thank you to him. He really was coming from a place of wanting to help me. I know that.)

And so getting on with it, we've already established or soon will establish that I am hilarious, mostly in my own head, but you get the picture.

I also love nerds and dorks and misfits.

I have opinions. Lord do I have opinions. Just ask my husband.

And just one word of advice for young readers out there. Right now, everyone in America is kind of loving a cowboy (thank you to the series *Yellowstone*, and yes, I'm with this group), but girls pay attention to the nerds too. You won't be sorry.

Nerds blossom too.

(Are they even called nerds anymore?)

I was going to start this book on January 12, 2024.

I'd been thinking about it for a while, you know?

It was to be a memoir.

The pieces and parts that stand out the most.

The highs and lows mostly because everything in the middle just gets well…lost.

The book was to be about the hardships I've endured, how unfair it's been, how difficult it has been. "Oh, woe is me."

I've wanted to talk about the struggles. You know, the struggles? The struggles every single one of us has in this life.

But now I've decided "Ain't nobody got time for that." (I think the lady who went viral for that had the last name of Brown? Thank you, Ms. Brown. I've been waiting for the perfect time to use it.)

I'd planned that my memoir was going to be about me.

Shocker, I know.

Before you set this book down or turn off the audio, just to open your electronics and mindlessly scroll. Just sit back, open your mind to possibilities, and just allow me to tell this story like Sandra Bullock's character "Margaret" when she fired "Bob Spaulding" in one of my favorite movies *The Proposal.*

I'm just going to tell this story the way that it happened in a calm and poised way.

It will be to the point and written in a matter-of-fact manner.

Although I'm starting pretty slow, this book is not ultimately about me at all.

Also, my apologies if this book seems to be less fluid than other memoirs out there. You will see why this book is written in the manner it is, in the upcoming pages.

We Need to Have Courage

I think that writing a memoir is one of the most courageous and brave things anyone can ever do in this life.

The vulnerability and humility it takes to put one's life out there on public display is incredibly difficult.

It is not for the faint of heart.

The critics are many.

They are literally everywhere.

They hide behind keyboards.

They let their fingers do their talking.

They say things with their keyboards that they would never say to someone's face. (Mike Tyson had it right when he said something like, "Some of you all getting too comfortable hiding behind a keyboard and not getting punched in the mouth." (Anyway, it was something like that.)

Mike Tyson had/has it right.

The critics are often the loudest voices in the room.

They speak over everyone else.

They want you to believe what they believe.

I think they are just "afraid."

It takes courage and speaking up for the critics to be silenced.

The critics are never standing in the arena.

Ever.

They are too scared to be vulnerable and open themselves up for attack.

The critics are so worried that you are going to see through them.

5

They forget we are all human beings. Imperfect in almost every single way possible.

So in starting this book again and again, it turns out I need a damn "calming goat" like "Lupe" from that movie and book *Ferdinand* for this whole book of what was going to be my memoir.

(God, I love that goat. She makes me laugh so much. I think, "I have got to channel my inner Lupe here. Lord help me find the words.")

The Build-Up

I'd had this idea in my head to write a book for a few years since I retired in 2014, but the timing was never quite right.

Although I was retired, I always seemed to be too busy.

I was too busy with my family, making house, doing life, raising animals, starting food blogs, stopping food blogs, taking care of my dear grandmother, and taking pictures.

I had begun taking a truckload of pictures. I took so many pictures I had to have more storage and memory on my devices.

Instead of just sitting back and observing, taking it all in and being present, I was always worried I had to capture the perfect shot to what? Show it off for the world?

Why did I do that?

Why do we do that?

Do you really think that Becky in Henderson Nevada actually cares that you made spaghetti for dinner or that you had a latte this morning?

(No offense to any Becky's out there. We've all seen what happened to poor Karen? And I do also love myself some latte so nothing is meant by that either. It's just a point.)

I'd often take ten photos of the same pose.

Do you do that too?

I began to wonder, *Why am I like this?*

My grandmother had a Polaroid camera that just took one picture at a time, and there was absolutely nothing wrong with that. It made photos much simpler.

At this point, I think I must have over thirty thousand photos on my phone. And if I add in the cameras of the past and the hard drives, memory cards, and old-school photo albums, it really becomes so overwhelming.

Photographs of life's sweetest and best memories should not feel "overwhelming."

I had to get the best shot, and I often thought, *Maybe one out of these ten shots in front of the Christmas tree will make my face angle a little thinner?*

The internal dialogue went something like this, "Chin out and down, twist the hips a little…hands on those hips…one leg forward and foot angled as if you are channeling your inner Victoria's Secret model."

Why do we think all of that is so important?

It's not.

What is important is that you have some photos of your friends and loved ones that you can enjoy and that make you smile when you look at them.

I began to think about the future and who would recognize any of my many photos in one hundred years. Would I ever have the time to go through the photos on my device and actually print out my favorites?

My mind went back to the photos of men and women my own grandmother had taken the time to save and protect over the years. She'd kept them in weatherproof bins in her garage, but she'd never had them out.

A large portion of all that remains of my grandmother's belongings are several large boxes of photo albums and framed photographs I don't want to throw out.

I know they were family members, but I still have no idea who almost all of those people are.

They were important enough for my grandmother to have kept and cherished over the years, and my gosh, they were actual photographs so they must be someone I should know.

But the sad thing was and continues to be…those photos might as well be photos of complete strangers because we never talked about any of them.

Most of them have only a first name written on the back of the photo.

I know one of the photos I have belongs to a man who was my great-great-grandfather named Charles Matthews.

I'd been told he'd changed his name to "Billy Smith" when he arrived in El Paso, Texas, in the late 1800s.

He was a professional boxer and one of El Paso's first police detectives.

He was even part of Theodore "Teddy" Roosevelt's Rough Riders. (The Rough Riders were comprised of people from many backgrounds, including law enforcement, cowboys, miners, athletes, etc. They handled "business" in creative ways.)

Again, my point is, photographs only have the importance that we, as individuals, place on them.

After my grandmother died and I suddenly became the owner of boxes full of photographs of people I didn't know, I started thinking about photographs more.

I'd think, *Do I want to leave my own children with this kind of responsibility?*

Do I want them to have any apprehension in keeping or parting with photographs of people they don't even know?

Maybe I need to think about streamlining photos, talking about family photographs, and labeling photographs with care for those I leave behind, etc.

In this section, I also want to talk about something I think should be discussed.

My mother struggled to keep the few cherished baby items she kept from my birth. She struggled to keep them because of her lifestyle and choices.

One of those sentimental items was my "baby book."

We used to keep baby books.

It was a way for people to celebrate the cherished life of a new baby and family member.

My mother kept a lock of my hair, my hospital bracelet, a list of gifts and gift givers, photos, teeth tracking…you name it.

When I was eighteen, I discovered that one of her landlords had taken my baby book, along with most of Mom's personal items, out to the middle of the Nevada desert and dumped them.

My mother hadn't returned to her studio apartment in some time and the landlord took matters into his own hands and emptied her apartment. I was told I showed up "one day too late."

I think, with all our photos and memories on devices, baby books may be overlooked these days by a lot of people.

I hope that changes.

When people close to us pass, their handwriting in baby books (and recipe books) becomes special to those they leave behind.

Who Am I?

Originally, in starting this book, I wanted to touch on some things that impacted me in my life. I know right? Get excited.

Born in Las Vegas, Nevada, my mom had been fifteen years old when she had me. Bless her heart.

She (and my father) didn't have any "Patience" (Guns N' Roses), and they both thought they were in "Heaven" (Kane Brown).

She wasn't even old enough to know who she was still developing into, let alone making the single most important life decision one will ever make in their lifetime.

I'm talking about who will become your husband and who will become the father of your children.

I'm not trying to badmouth my father.

He did the best he absolutely could too.

I have nothing but love for him.

What I'm saying is that somewhere along the line in history, women have forgotten. Women have completely forgotten that they are in charge of who they allow into their lives in an intimate way.

They get to decide.

It is a decision that must be thought out and weighed.

How much time do you listen to that person chewing? Do you like the sound of their voice? Do they have any ambition at all? What are their goals? Do they even have any? Are they into good hygiene? What are their views on having and raising children? The questions should go on and on.

If a woman allows someone into their life in an intimate way, it doesn't even matter if there is ultimately a marriage.

If a baby is produced from a woman allowing someone to be intimate with her, she will essentially be married to that other person whether on paper or not for the rest of that baby's life and maybe beyond.

Sidebar on Nature

I'm trying not to get ahead of my skis here, but this is also something that I think can benefit people.

It is a different perspective.

Since I moved to a more rural area and am now surrounded by a ton of farm animals and wildlife, I've made observations that I'd like to share with everyone.

I think that the animal kingdom and human beings have more in common than we think.

I guess because I'd never been exposed to animals other than a family dog or cat, I didn't know how hard the male animal species has to work to get a female's attention in the wild.

Let's take a bird for example. Many of the birds around my home start mating in the spring. The male birds are covered in very elaborate and bright feathers, and most of the female birds are very neutral in color. The male birds have all the elaborate colors so that they can attract the females.

Wild turkeys (not the alcohol) are a bird that I see very often at my home.

The turkeys travel in large flocks during winter for safety.

They sleep in the cottonwood trees at night to avoid land predators.

They leave "turkey poop popsicles" all over my property. (Then my dogs get sick eating those popsicles, but that's for another time. Oh, how I love "turkey poop popsicles.")

My point is, the male turkey in spring actually competes with all the other male turkeys. At other times during the year, the males group up and walk around, not bothering each other or any of the female turkeys.

But when spring comes and it's time to mate with a female, it is "game on."

Those male turkeys inherently know they must "bring it" if they are going to be her top choice to father her baby turkey "chicks."

Those male turkeys know they must compete for the females.

Those male turkeys know they must compete for the female's attention.

The male turkey will puff up his chest as big as he possibly can around the females. His head, neck, and "waddle" will suddenly turn bright colors of red, lavender, and blue. It's actually quite something to see.

The wild male turkey transforms from this average-looking large feathered brown bird into something almost unrecognizable from his former appearance when it's time to mate.

He will begin to strut around trying to get a female hen to notice him. He will fight and struggle with the other males in an attempt to show the female how big and strong he is.

The struggles the male turkeys participate in can actually be quite brutal.

But the dominant male turkey will do this to show her that he should be the one turkey that is "allowed" to mate with her.

She gets to choose her mate, and they both know it.

Mom

Continued

So my apologies for the detour in my story about wild turkeys, but again, my point is that my mother was only fifteen, and she didn't even pause to make a choice.

She just went along to get along.

She wasn't taught how to choose anything from a young age. Do you want water, or do you want milk? Would you like to go to bed now or in five minutes? Would you like to turn off the television or would you like me to do it?

(All these basic things we often just tell our children to do should be things that we ask our children to decide for themselves when provided choices we, as parents, approve of while they are young. How are they ever going to begin actually using their own brains if we don't allow them to make easy choices and possibly fail while they are young?)

Because she was never actually taught how to make choices at a young age when those choices were not going to impact her life in a significant way…how in the world was my mother supposed to make the most important choice she would ever make in her entire life at fifteen?

I only lived with mom for the first seven years of my life but the first seven are so important in a child's life.

She tried so hard.

She really did.

She was a fighter too.

She did the best she knew how to do with me, but there were so many things that happened that should not happen to a child or in front of a child.

These are the things I originally wanted to write about in a memoir.

So that you may understand my personality a little more, I will explain just a little about who I was from a young age.

At the age of four, I walked home by myself from the preschool bus that dropped me off at my apartment complex where I lived with my mom. The apartment complex was on a street called Swenson in Las Vegas and very close to the Las Vegas Strip.

By the age of five, I was waking myself up at five or six in the morning, grabbing something to eat, and walking to school by myself to hang out on the swings before the teachers even arrived.

I'm guessing the school was half a mile to a mile away.

I'd often walked to school alone in the dark.

At one point, I remember walking home from school, and I found my mom crying in the living room. She yelled at me and blamed me for a break-in that happened after I left for school.

She'd said I'd left the door to the apartment unlocked, and someone came in and stole the gold chain off her neck and a lot of other things including our clothes iron.

I remember feeling so terrible. I didn't mean to leave the door unlocked. I cried after she yelled at me, and I felt like I was an inch tall.

I think, but I'm not quite sure, that Child Protective Services was also called on one occasion because I was often at the school too early, alone.

By the age of seven, my grandparents stepped in to raise me.

There were a few bumps until I was eighteen but nothing I even need to mention here.

My grandparents also did the very best they knew how to raise me.

My Career

I started testing for the Las Vegas Metropolitan Police Department at the age of seventeen and was fortunate enough to be hired at eighteen directly after high school.

Up until that point, I had been a lifeguard at the Mirage Hotel and Casino on the Las Vegas Strip for three summers.

I was so excited to receive a call back to work after that first summer, and I'll never forget that phone call from one of the pool managers named "Kevin" who made that call to me to see if I wanted to come back another summer to work at that beautiful lagoon-style pool.

That was the best job ever!

I get nostalgic when I hear a Jimmy Buffet song like "Cheeseburger in Paradise" or Andrea Bocelli's "Con te partiro."

Those were just a couple of songs that wafted through the air on the daily from the carefully placed speakers around the pool.

I absolutely loved that job except for that time I fell off the life-guard platform/stand in more than fifty-mile-an-hour winds trying to take down a very heavy wood-framed umbrella over my stand before it flew off and impaled a guest of the hotel.

The winds had been so strong that warm sunny morning that the umbrella began to lift out of its "seating" behind my lifeguard chair.

As I tried to close the canopy of the umbrella, the whole thing began to fly away, and I remember thinking, *Uh-oh, a guest is going to get hurt and I'm actually going to fall off this lifeguard stand right now. Yep, it's happening.*

I'd landed right on my back on the pool decking.

I had been standing straight up under the umbrella while trying to remove the pin that kept the canopy open.

The actual lifeguard platform I'd been standing on was also about six feet off the ground, and I stood almost six feet tall myself.

I fell hard and couldn't even breathe from the pain.

As I just lay on the pool decking at the "baby pool" grabbing at my back and consumed with lower back pain, a man who'd been lounging at the pool came over and asked me what he should do.

I breathed, "blow my whistle hard."

He did. Other lifeguards came running, and I was ultimately transported to the nearest emergency room via ambulance where a multitude of tests were run.

I was bruised very badly, but I recovered from the fall and returned to work shortly after.

I'm not sure what happened to the flying umbrella.

I left the Mirage Pool in late June 1992 and began working for the Las Vegas Metropolitan Police Department in July 1992.

I worked for the police department for twenty-two years, and I progressed to the rank of police lieutenant over the years.

I was a woman in an "alpha" male environment and I often felt underestimated and misunderstood.

I was highly introverted but also highly capable. Never the loudest voice in the room, I was often quiet but extremely observant.

I didn't miss a thing that happened in any room or any meeting.

I was one who would take it all in and then go and get the work done when it actually needed to be done.

I knew that I had strengths and talents that made me special. It was important to me to be taken seriously.

Over the course of seventeen years with the police department, I'd worked very hard, and I'd made it to my dream job.

My dream job had been to be in charge of the Special Victim's Section.

I loved that show with Mariska Hargitay and Christopher Meloni called Law and Order-Special Victims Unit (SVU).

I can still hear the music that was used for the series.

I loved that job so much.

I had this belief that I could really do some good there both for the section and for the victims of the types of crimes we'd investigate under that section of the department.

I'd always believed that so much good could come from investigating crimes that victimized our most vulnerable (children and elderly).

I ultimately retired from the police department in 2014.

By in large, I'd loved working for that agency.

I loved the feeling of pride in that uniform, even as uncomfortable as it was.

Thirty pounds of gear is no joke on a back and neck over time.

I loved some of the people I'd worked with.

If you ever want to hear some funny things, a briefing room is the place to be.

Just people being people.

And despite what anyone tells you, "cops" have the best and sometimes the most dark senses of humor. It's really a product of the job.

I found they'd often used humor as a coping tool to regroup after some of the things they'd witnessed and actually had to deal with in humanity throughout their shifts. They'd decompress in the "briefing room" before going home to their families or anyone else. Those are the kinds of things I miss about the police department.

I miss some of those people I worked with as well.

Some of those men were the most big-hearted, well-meaning, articulate, integrity-filled people I have ever met.

After I retired, I moved to Montana and settled in with my husband and that's where I've spent the last ten years of my life.

It has been quite the opposite life from the one I lived in Las Vegas.

Over the years, when I'd think about writing this book, I always had one story that popped into my mind, and I'd always wanted it to be the first story in my book.

It was a touching moment between two strangers, and I don't think I'll ever forget it.

It went like this:

I'd been the lieutenant over Special Victims for a few weeks.

I felt so amazing.

I remember practically strutting through that Clark County Courthouse building.

Fierce. I mean, fierce.

That's the way I felt anyway.

I was so proud of who I was and what I'd become in this life.

I was riding a high only personal accomplishment could produce.

I was just so proud of me.

I loved who I'd become.

I remember I was wearing a dark navy blue suit, a crisp white button-up shirt underneath my fitted suit jacket, and reasonable but feminine high heels.

(Dark colors always made me feel more powerful. I'd learned the power of color when testing for promotion to police sergeant and then again with my testing for promotion to police lieutenant. I'd loved softer colors, but I knew that darker colors not only made one feel more influential and authoritative but the people who would be analyzing my performance on the promotional boards were also influenced by color. I knew if I wore a lighter and softer color to a promotional board in which I was competing with mostly men, I'd be seen as possibly being "soft" or "weak.")

At the courthouse, I walked into the office of a man who I knew to be a deputy district attorney "boss."

I don't remember the official title he held but you know? "The guy in charge, numero uno, the head honcho," if you will.

He was this "teddy bear" type man with graying brown hair and eyeglasses.

He was in his late fifties or early sixties, I'd guessed.

He'd been sitting in the warm yellow glow of the sun at his desk when I peeked my head in to see if he was there in his office.

I tapped on his door and walked in so that I could introduce myself.

I knew we'd be working together, and I'd been in the building, so I stopped in to say hello.

He stood up when he saw me.

I walked over to him and held out my hand to shake his.

I told him my name was "Kasey Matthews" and that I was happy to meet him.

I explained that I was the new section commander/lieutenant over Metro's Special Victim's Section.

The man's hand was big like a mitt as he shook my hand back.

He smiled and got this strange look on his face.

He paused.

He spoke softly and asked me if I was related to "Jack Matthews, the real estate businessman in town?"

I was so pleased he knew my grandfather.

I smiled and said quickly, "Yes, he was my grandfather. He died a few years ago. Why do you ask?"

He paused again but pressed further.

"How are you related to Jack's son Jon?"

Now I was confused.

I had never met this man but he seemed to know my family tree pretty well.

I didn't talk much about my family tree to anyone outside of my small circle of about oh, one person, and she had been my best friend since we were fifteen to sixteen years old.

A bit taken aback, I just decided to be honest.

I said, "Jon is my father."

Now he was clearly uncomfortable.

Man, this guy paused a lot, I thought.

He proceeded but seemed to choose his words carefully.

He said something like, "You know, I was a young deputy district attorney thirty or so years ago. I was newly graduated from law school."

He went on, "Jon was one of the first people I ever prosecuted… for arson."

He almost seemed to be asking a question when he added the word *arson*.

After another thoughtful pause, he said, "You know, Jon always maintained in trial that he'd burned down his brother-in-law's place because he'd been sexually molesting his [Jon's] daughter."

He stopped.

He just looked at me.

I had the quick flash of a mental picture.

I thought, *Why do I need to be ashamed of this? I am not the one who did anything wrong.*

I had a quick flash of memory.

The memory was a picture of my small four-year-old hands as they were trying to unlock the brass bolted lock on a white door.

My hands were trying to unlock the door to run away.

I said simply, in a matter-of-fact manner, "Well, he was telling the truth. He did burn that place down because my uncle molested me."

Later, I'd think back on this and know, "Jon, my father, sacrificed part of his life and his own freedom for me. He loved me unconditionally, as a father is supposed to."

No one ever needs to be ashamed of a father's love.

COVID-19 *and the Aftermath*

I think since the onset of COVID-19, I started becoming this… person.

This person I just didn't like at all.

My grandmother died on January 23, 2020, at the age of eighty-nine, five days after her birthday. Losing her was very hard on me.

I'd lived a season of about five years that was very stressful on me as her primary caretaker.

I carried a lot of guilt about how difficult and frustrating I was finding it to watch her age.

I watched her go from a strong, proud, "doctorate" educated woman to this frail, dependent shell of her former self.

I found myself mourning her while she was alive as I watched all the pieces and parts of who she was: fall away to age.

I think watching the people we love grow old is not really talked about enough.

Some caretakers are very tired, detached, and dragging at times like newborn baby parents.

In the end, what our aging family members need is really just some grace.

They need to be cared for respectfully, and they need us to understand that and be comfortable with that.

They need grace to just relax and fall into what is meant to be… eventually for all of us.

I miss my grandmother so much. I took so much for granted.

My grandmother had a fall and died a couple of days later in a hospice care facility.

And soon, all things COVID-19 hit and engulfed the world into this…well, nightmare.

It seems like it's been a nightmare for the past three solid years.

The world has been crying since the onset of COVID-19 in my opinion.

As COVID-19 consumed the world, I quickly became this stressed-out, anxious, chip-on-my-shoulder person.

Even after the doom and gloom started to subside somewhat, I was trying to do all the things I was supposed to do every day.

Make the bed, pick up the bathroom towels, do the laundry, clean the sink off, do the dishes, be a self-proclaimed Uber driver— on and on it went.

I was feeling like the maid. A paler, taller, and sadly less-voluptuous version of the beautiful Jennifer Lopez (J-Lo) in that romantic feel-good movie *Maid in Manhattan*.

COVID-19 really changed us. It changed how we treated each other.

Everyone was and they continue to be so stressed out.

People are short-tempered.

They don't like to make eye contact.

People won't even offer to help an older lady with her groceries or mow her lawn, let alone offer to chop some firewood for her so that she can be warm in winter.

These thoughts apply to older men as well.

Older men need help too.

They've grown up in a time when they were supposed to be strong and take care of everything.

They may never ask for help because of pride.

These things that we do every day and grumble about are very difficult for the elderly.

If you decide to do any of these things after reading or listening to this book, just remember to show the elderly some "grace."

They may not respond like you think or hope they will, but try anyway.

Personally, after COVID-19, I began to consume social media in a way that was so severely detrimental to my well-being.

I was listening to podcasts and watching videos every single day. I'd consume the material in my kitchen, my living room, folding laundry, driving in my car, you name it.

The podcasts and videos I sought to hear and see were full of negative information and news about almost everything that could go wrong or would go wrong.

I would tune into them every single day.

I began listening to confirm what I already knew in my heart.

We do that, don't we?

We seek out information that only serves to validate our current belief system.

We have really become masters of that.

I am embarrassed to say that I even knew the typical release times for some of those podcasts that were released every single day.

In fact, I couldn't wait to have some "alone" time to absorb more.

Why did I do that?

I realize that this does not apply to everyone out there, but I also know I am not alone.

There are people in this world just trying to put food on the table.

There are people out there who are just trying to feed their kids.

There are people who are just scraping by to pay their bills.

There are people just trying to handle all of their adulting responsibilities while also trying to stay healthy, and just, well… survive.

By the time I reached January of this year (2024), I had migrated from podcasts and videos to what I'll call social media "scroll fests."

I would literally waste about four to eight hours a day. It didn't happen every day, but it happened enough to make me very unhappy with how I was spending my free time.

"Surely that can't be correct?"

"Sometimes four to eight hours?"

I'd limit my device time significantly, and still, the analytics told me four to eight hours?

"No, that can't be right?" I'd think.

So to manage the guilt I'd felt for wasting all that time, I'd simply turn off the notifications. I chose not to see the amount of time I was wasting in my life on things that didn't really matter.

While I did start to look for more hope in podcasts, like Joel Osteen and Mel Robbins, and self-improvement and leadership sessions with John Maxwell during 2023, it wasn't enough to stop the constant time-wasting activities I'd allowed myself to engage in.

I'd always felt strong, you know?

I could take it or leave it.

I was still lying in bed at night.

I was unable to sleep, the light of my device in my face, trying to consume the garbage and not wake my husband.

I was actually ashamed I was doing that in our bed.

I'd plug my device in next to the bed on the floor and try to sleep.

I'd wake up in the middle of the night, grab my device again, and it went on and on.

In the morning, the device was the first thing I reached for.

Around five o'clock most mornings, I'd try to sneak out of bed so as not to wake my husband.

I'd go downstairs to have some "private" scroll time with my device.

My husband would come downstairs in the morning, and instead of being happy to see him, I'd be annoyed that I had to put my device down.

I should have been enjoying our quiet time together, but I was not.

I was obsessed with my device.

I'd spend my evenings after dinner on the couch, scrolling as well.

I was only seeing the best and the worst of others on my screen, and while I tried to be present with my family, I was never really intentional about our evenings together.

Why was I doing this?

I'd racked up hundreds and hundreds of emails I never looked at through "subscriptions" I didn't need.

I began to avoid looking at my email because that became too overwhelming as well.

When I did have a moment to go into my email and "unsubscribe" from whatever I felt wasn't "serving" my needs any longer, I'd often find it difficult to find the "unsubscribe" on the screen, and even better yet, there wasn't one!

More time wasted.

And can someone please talk about the amount of passwords we are all carrying around in our heads, written in little books or worse yet, saved on our devices?

Lord, please make it stop.

What character did I use there?

Was the letter a capital or lowercase?

The dog or the cat's name, and what year was it?

How many old cords to devices do you have? I have a shoebox full of old cords "just in case" I need to get into an old device. These things take up space in our homes. They take up space in our minds. They take up space in our hearts.

Do you have a drawer or a shoe box? Which one is it?

I used to know all my friend's phone numbers by heart.

I still remember my childhood home number from age seven on 871-4344.

Now I am ashamed to say I don't even require my brain to memorize almost all numbers of those people closest to me.

What do people even do if they are booked into jail now?

I was crabby, snappy, and complaining all the time.

Did I not think that my husband knew how to drive already?

Had he been driving for years before I met him without any assistance from me? Yep.

Not going to lie here. I will probably still do this. I never said I was perfect.

And then there was "dinner" or "supper" or whatever you call it in your house.

Every day, the "what's for dinner" subject would come up.

Again? "Awe, man, I just fed you people last night. You want to eat again?"

I loved to cook, and I'd become quite accomplished at it, but doing it every night felt like a job and I was not enjoying it at all.

I always felt like another saying floating around out there about, "Being responsible for every meal for every person, every day for the rest of my life until I die…"

Yeah, it kind of felt like that.

I wanted to enjoy cooking again.

Meals with your family are to be cherished. I knew this.

As I made meals in our beautiful kitchen (a kitchen I am grateful to have), I would get easily annoyed by my dogs.

They are complete food nuts.

You know the kind?

They hear a cheese wrapper coming off or a hard-boiled egg cracking and they are immediately standing next to me.

They stand "front and center" in the position of "attention."

Their "puppy dog" eyes looked expectantly and longingly at me.

They patiently wait for just a morsel of food to fall so they can quickly grab it up.

Nothing makes them happier than an unexpected snack.

They are larger dogs and larger dogs can be a problem in the kitchen.

I'd frequently be in the middle of making a meal and turn quickly to move somewhere else in the kitchen.

I was always trying to be overly efficient and do things too quickly.

I'd be at the kitchen sink and turn without looking, nearly falling over the dogs.

They were just doing what some dogs do.

I was starting to act like the dad in one of my favorite Christmas movies *A Christmas Story*. Remember him yelling, "Bumpuses!" after they'd stolen his precious turkey or when he'd come home from work?

Yeah, it was kind of like that for a while around my kitchen. "Bumpuses!" That term had become a running joke in our house.

I began to worry about everything like I was trying to make it an Olympic sport.

I was fantastic at it.

I'm guessing there are a ton of women (and men) out there who also worry about every single thing that can go wrong.

Why was I doing this?

I knew that worrying had the same effect on the human body as if the very thing one worried about actually happened.

I was hurting my entire being with "worry" about things that weren't even within my control.

As I neared my January birthday and the half century milestone, I started to have problems seeing anything up close with my glasses on.

I'd never had a problem seeing anything close up in my entire life, so this vision issue, along with the diagnoses of a couple of cataracts at age forty-eight, were tough to take.

I remember looking at the optometrist when he broke the news to me about the cataracts.

I said, "But cataracts are for old people."

The optometrist said, "Well, these are not the same type of cataracts that the older population usually develop."

I looked at him and thought, *Cute. Way to try to soften the blow.*

His comment did not help one iota.

So to be able to see up close, I'd begun to take my glasses off throughout the day while I walked around the house looking at my device.

I'd take the glasses off, sometimes positioning them on top of my head so that I could look at whatever "notification" saw fit to interrupt my day.

It happened constantly.

One notification on my device of some news story that I could do absolutely nothing about turned into another and turned into a swipe, a click, and an hour down the drain.

I walk around the house literally looking for the pair of glasses on top of my head multiple times a day!

Devices and Unnecessary Stuff

I started making way too many purchases of things I didn't need, never needed, and won't ever need in this lifetime.

I'd also receive multiple "status" updates via email about the unnecessary items I'd order. Did I really need several updates cluttering my email to say my cardboard box (in a cardboard box) was "shipped" or that it was "on the way?"

No. I think my day would go on just fine without those extra notifications.

The boxes came way too often, and I was ashamed.

I'd seen those statements out there on floor mats or other items that said something like, "Dear delivery driver, hide the packages from my husband."

While I never did that, I felt that statement on many levels.

I was accumulating stuff I didn't need, and I felt miserable about it.

I'd started to think toward the end of 2023 that I was drowning in stuff in my own house.

I'd leave my basket of folded laundry in my bedroom and not put it away.

I dreaded putting laundry away because guess what? I didn't have any space in my closets or drawers to put things away easily because I had too many clothes I didn't even wear.

I started thinking, *Is my house going to fall apart if I don't follow the latest trend?*

Why do I even care what the latest and greatest trend is anyway?

Does a gold-colored faucet trend affect my life in any way? Do I need to change my home and follow the whims of others and the influence of marketing to feel good in my home?

No. Not at all.

I needed to do better.

All these things started coming to my mind in 2023.

I'd start wondering, *Why do I bring my device everywhere I go?*

When I'd drive with my family in the car, I'd think, *Why do I need my device too if I know another adult has one?*

Didn't people survive just fine for decades in cars without any device at all?

Do I not think that if there is an emergency somewhere, one device in the car will probably be sufficient?

Does my family have my husband's phone number if they really need to get ahold of me?

Can we miss one call?

How many automated messages do we get these days?

If the device buzzes or chimes, why do I stop what I'm doing to look at it?

Is it that important?

If I miss a robocall, am I gonna make it through the day? You bet.

I started to notice myself getting to school or appointments early just to do the "scroll."

I had to keep up with everything I thought was important.

But was it really important?

Could I have spent that time cleaning out some more of my closet, donating to the truly needy, or doing anything else other than sitting in my car wasting precious time?

I knew when I was supposed to be there.

Grown adults know how to be on time.

I'd also started to let people take advantage of me.

I was allowing this to happen way too often, and I knew I needed to start setting some boundaries quickly.

I just started getting to the point in 2023 that I didn't need to do all that anymore.

I'm not naive. I realize that so much of our lives and businesses are interconnected with a device of some sort. It is just the way it is.

But still, I knew I could do better.

I was out of the work grind at this point in life, but as a leader in a law enforcement environment, I'd read about the problem of employees being "absent on the job."

No one's toilet habits are any of my business, but I'd laughed to myself and thought I wonder if "toilet reading" is seriously impacting the workforce now?

And lastly, I'd really started ignoring my health. I made a lot of excuses.

Sugar Cookies

They're Not Just for Christmas

I'd taken up sugar cookie art in January 2023 for a family bridal shower in July ('23). I'd been searching for something to bring out my creativity, and I quickly loved it. The sugar cookie hobby also helped me to separate myself more from my device, and I grew to love the act of creating "special" cookies very quickly.

I'd really just started cookies to surprise a "special" bride. I wanted to show her that I'd taken the time to learn this skill just for her event. I wanted to make her feel like, you know, a bride.

Never a "stick a toe in" kind of girl, I began collecting all the tools and toys I thought I needed to improve my sugar cookie decorating game.

That sugar cookie life is quite something.

I'd traveled to my first cookie con (a yearly cookie convention) in Orlando, Florida, in August 2023.

I absolutely loved it.

I felt so inspired.

I kind of had this thought, *These are my people*, as I took in the instructional classes and meandered around the vending hall.

The bridal event I'd begun practicing for came and went.

But still, I continued.

I found the art of icing cookies to be very soothing and therapeutic.

I loved the videos online of the act of simply adding icing fluidly to a sugar cookie.

Those videos felt so satisfying to watch.

I practiced making and decorating my sugar cookies for almost a year, leading up to my fiftieth birthday.

People started asking me if I was going to sell my cookies, but I knew I didn't want to make a job out of something I loved to do.

I also didn't want to disappoint actual customers if my cookie creations weren't what they'd envisioned.

I'd had this thought that I may teach classes in the future just to share the therapeutic side of cookies with other people as well.

Pilates

In an effort to kick-start my 2024 new year, I signed up for some Pilates classes in November 2023.

I loved it immediately.

My instructor was a bubbly, cheerful, positive, and petite blonde in her early fifties.

I'd used Pilates to help find another outlet away from my device.

Pilates made me feel great, and I began to enjoy working out again. I also saw Pilates as a healthier way to spend my time instead of gravitating toward my device.

The Birthday

Throughout the year 2023, I'd think about the fact that I was turning fifty in January 2024.

Along with all the consumption of garbage, I'd willingly let myself take in daily for years, I began really struggling with the milestone birthday for about three months leading up to it.

I had become more agitated than what had become usual in the three years post-COVID-19.

I worried that my worth would somehow be less because of my looming new age.

I'd started thinking about how fast ten years had gone. It had literally gone by in the blink of an eye.

You know that saying "Life is like a roll of toilet paper. The quicker it gets to the end, the quicker it goes?"

Well, I was feeling that.

In my forties, I'd put on a few extra pounds as a lot of us do.

My lifestyle changed completely at age forty, and it had an effect on my health.

The pounds bothered me, though.

I mean, we are lucky and should be grateful to grow older and to afford food that brings those pesky weight-influencing calories to our plates.

(You know that strange thing called a "calorie," right? The little boogers go in and sew your clothes tighter while you're sleeping.)

Yeah, those things.

I'd been easily able to keep the pounds off in my younger years, but I'd begun to feel the pounds really weighing on me. Get it? I call myself a "dork" for a reason.

Society is so completely obsessed and opinionated about what is acceptable and what is not.

This is just my opinion, but I've always felt that women, especially women, are held to this higher standard of beauty as they fight the aging process with every cream, concoction, and spa treatment.

I was and continue to be guilty of this myself.

That may never stop as we try to continue "self-care" and to be gentle with ourselves. It is okay to take care of yourself.

But my point is, men get more "distinguished" in age while women…well, we just get old.

Men get a Corvette at fifty, and women get a younger-looking hairstyle and a self-help book.

Male actors in their fifties get a starring role with a younger female lead in her twenties while female actresses get the role of "grandmother" at fifty.

For me, as "fifty" approached, I was starting to fear becoming this "invisible" person.

I'd read a statement somewhere in my life that stayed with me.

I'd often thought about it while taking care of my grandmother as she aged.

The statement said something like, "The old woman is the least often looked at person in America. We ignore her. We pretend she doesn't exist as we move through our lives at the grocery store…," and so on.

After I read that, I'd always tried to be intentional about looking into the faces of the old women I encountered.

They were mothers, sisters, daughters, wives, partners, aunts, and grandmothers.

I'm sure I'm missing some important titles, but my whole point is, those women are human beings and they matter.

We should never pretend they don't exist or avoid eye contact with them.

We need to show them some grace.

Also, during the 2023 year, as I inched my way to "fifty," I had the fortunate or unfortunate (depending on how you look at aging) onset of that big M thing called menopause.

"Mood Swings. Available every ten minutes."

I'd been going through that extra fun time of menopause, and I finally knew what all these ladies from my past had been talking about.

Once a very young lady, I'd listened to that kind of talk before. It never applied to me until it did.

I'd just shrugged my shoulders and thought, *Well, those are just the rantings of Golden Girl types.* (Note: I miss the comedy of Betty White. The world needs more comedy.)

I'd think, *None of that menopause stuff is my issue, so I'm not gonna give it another thought.*

My amazing best friend and I were living way too far apart during this time in 2023.

I wanted her to be close, but alas, our paths had gone different ways after we both moved out of Las Vegas in 2012 and 2014 respectively.

We'd met in a high school gym while we were fifteen and training for volleyball. (Truly, the best sport ever in my opinion.)

Our hang-out time happened via telephone mostly.

We were/are the kind of ladies who send funny statements to each other that we find on the Internet of Things.

We'd send each other messages with the words, "Finally shaved my legs and donated it all to locks of love," or "My summer bikini body wasn't ready, but my fall sweater body is on point."

One of our absolute favorites was the photo of Minnie from the movie *The Help*. She's holding that pie—you know the one (the poo-poo pie).

The photo had words on it that said something like, "Some days you just feel like baking someone a pie."

That photo of Minnie holding that pie while dressed in her Sunday best seemed to be funnier and funnier every time we shared a new version of it.

There were always plenty of versions floating around to be plucked right off social.

Menopause Continued

We'd chat on the phone, comparing our symptoms.

It went something like this, "Oh my, I have had the sweats something fierce girl. I literally have to change my sheets every night."

Or "Hubs can sleep through a damn fire alarm going off. Why can't I sleep?"

And "Oh yeah, well my ear canals itch. What the heck is that all about?"

And I can't forget the "I feel nauseous all the time. Lord, make it stop!"

Well, that nauseous one was actually me, but seriously (another shameless *The Help* plug), I felt like that Ms. Hilley character in the movie after she found out that she'd eaten Minnie's poop.

No one actually told me nausea was a thing in menopause.

I'd thought that was a special treat only reserved for women lucky enough to get pregnant.

(Note: I know not everyone agrees with this. It's a personal thing. I, however, love babies, felt like I actually glowed in pregnancy, and if I could have another I would.)

The Whole Point of this Memoir

Thanks for hanging in there until this point.

Now some of this will be super important.

So strap yourselves in and open your minds.

It starts slow but gets better.

In the summer of July 2017, I began to feel ill one day.

I was doing some online shopping for things I absolutely did not need, and I spent the afternoon lying on the couch, trying to feel better.

I went to sleep that night, still not feeling quite right.

I woke up the next day, still feeling a little ill.

I walked downstairs and put some essential oils under my tongue to try to help with the nauseous feeling I was having.

I told my husband I wasn't feeling well, and I went back upstairs for a nap.

I took about an hour nap, but I still wasn't feeling much better.

Thinking I'd eaten something that caused some food poisoning, I placed a trashcan from the bathroom next to my bed…just in case.

I remember my husband coming in to check on me several times throughout the day as I tried to sleep.

Sometime during the day, my stomach began to hurt in my right lower quadrant.

My husband let me rest, and day turned into night.

I remember having the "sweats" and not sleeping at all that night. I tossed and turned most of the night, trying to get comfortable.

The night turned into day again.

At about the twenty-four-hour mark in bed, I was struggling to get comfortable and trying to rest most of the time. I continued to try to shake off whatever was wrong with me.

I remember looking at the clock at around 10:00 a.m.

The intense pain I'd been feeling in my stomach suddenly stopped around that time.

I was so relieved that I quickly fell back asleep, happy the pain had subsided.

Looking back now, I do believe that the pain of what I was enduring was so intense that I'd gone into some sort of shock.

I wasn't communicating like I should with my husband.

I vaguely remember him coming through our bedroom a few times the second day to check on me.

He came in around that 10:00 a.m. hour, and I told him I'd felt that the pain in my stomach had subsided. He'd been very happy to hear that, and I think we both thought this illness would be over soon.

I fell back asleep sometime after that, but I woke up suddenly in extreme pain again in the afternoon.

I fumbled for my device to call my best friend. She'd lost two mothers to cancer and she'd made it her mission to understand nutrition and health after the incredible losses. I knew this, and that is why I called her at that moment.

After I reached her, I told her what had been happening.

I was trying to hide my real condition and not scare her.

I told her I was in a lot of pain, and I thought I'd had food poisoning.

The conversation is very blurry, but I remember her telling me that maybe some "charcoal" would help if it had been food poisoning. (The kind of charcoal sold in stores and pharmacy areas.)

At the end of the conversation, I remember her saying, "Promise me…absolutely promise me you will go to the emergency room if it doesn't go away."

My husband gave me some charcoal capsules and water, and I quickly fell back asleep.

At about three o'clock in the morning, I woke up again.

I was drenched in sweat, and I could barely move.

I was in such unbelievable pain I cannot even describe it.

At that point in those dark morning hours, I'd been battling this sudden illness for forty-one hours or so.

My husband had not slept very well the night before, and he wanted to give me my space to get better, so he had gone to another room to sleep for the night.

I literally had to peel myself off the bed at that moment. It took every bit of strength I had left to try to stand up. It turns out that I couldn't.

I got down on all fours and began crawling to my bedroom door. I was crying and just trying to make it to the hallway so I could cry out for my husband down the hall.

At one point, my dog Lilly came up the stairs. She must have heard me moving around and thought it odd at that time of morning.

She met me just outside my doorway in the hallway.

She began pushing her nose in my face, nudging me to see if I was okay.

No, Lilly. I was not okay. I was calling out for my husband and trying to crawl past Lilly and her efforts to help me with her cold wet nose.

And like that song by Charlie Puth "One Call Away," I cried out loud enough for my husband to hear…finally.

He came running down the hall.

The Hospital

Thirty minutes later, my husband got me out of the car and inside the check-in area of the emergency room closest to us.

I remember being grateful there was no one else in the check-in/ waiting area.

He helped me into the hospital through the automatic doors as I could only walk with assistance.

The woman behind the check-in counter took one look at me, holding my abdomen, stood up, and said, "Stomach?"

All I could do at that point was nod.

I could barely speak.

She found a wheelchair somewhere, and the next thing I knew, I was being wheeled into an examination room in the emergency room.

Once I arrived in an examination room, I remember a female nurse who was probably in her late fifties or early sixties. She asked me to get out of the wheelchair and onto the hospital bed in the room.

I literally could not do this. There was no way that was going to happen.

I held my arm up for her to help me.

She muttered something about not being able to help me onto the bed because of a back injury. (It could have been a neck injury? This is very blurry in my memory.)

At that time, I believe a male nurse came into the room. He was like a knight in shining armor to me at that moment. He helped me onto the hospital bed.

He later told me his name was Matt.

I remember Matt being so patient with me as I writhed around in pain on that hospital bed. He was trying to take my blood pressure and all the other necessities I barely remember.

I remember a young male doctor coming into the room.

He'd had short blond hair.

He asked me some questions.

I remember him telling me he was ordering some kind of test to look at my stomach.

The doctor left the room at some point with Nurse Matt.

The female nurse began asking me questions at one point.

She'd held a clipboard and a pen and began verbally firing away from across the small room.

Now looking back on this, I realize I must have looked like a nightmare. At forty-one hours in, my hair was a mess, my clothes were drenched in sweat, I probably stunk to high heaven, and I'm lying in the woman's examination room with some unexplained stomach pain.

Her questions started out simple enough.

"Name, known allergies."

But then she got to the question about drugs.

She asked me if I'd used any drugs.

"No," I sputtered. "No drugs."

Then she went on to "alcohol."

Now I did love myself some "Red Red Wine" with dinner, so I told her, "Yeah, a few days ago with dinner."

Still consumed with pain at that point and barely able to breathe, I really tried not to get angry at her next question.

Obviously not believing me about the drugs, she asked me a second time.

"Have you used any drugs?"

I remember wanting to come off that table at her at that very moment.

I actually pictured punching her in her throat across the room like Elastigirl from the *Incredibles* but using Mr. Incredibles's fist.

After that, I remember being wheeled down some hallway to another examination room with some space-age-looking equipment.

I was asked if I could turn on my side. I guess I did. I don't remember now.

At some point, I was back in the examination room with Nurse Matt.

I remember him telling me the doctor was just waiting for the results of the test and then I could probably have some pain medicine.

He said I just needed to "hang in there."

I remember this next statement so very clearly.

I knew I was dying on that table, and I asked Matt to tell the doctor to please hurry.

Nurse Matt left the room after that.

I'm not sure how much time passed between my asking Nurse Matt to tell the doctor to hurry and his actual return to the exam room, but at some point, the doctor returned to my room.

He told me that he'd seen the results of the test, and he'd found out that my appendix had ruptured.

He mentioned a word called *sepsis* and said something about "emergency surgery" and "the surgeon is on her way."

I remember at some point after that, Nurse Matt administered pain medication through an IV.

I believe I fell asleep shortly after that.

I remember waking up partially and seeing Nurse Matt pushing my hospital bed through the hallways and on an elevator in the hospital.

Shortly after this memory of Nurse Matt, I recall a room where there were several hospital employees.

They wore face masks and blue gowns.

I remember one of them asking me if I could get myself onto the surgery table.

I tried, but I could not.

I remember a face mask with a suction sound coming from it being placed over my face.

And then everything went dark.

The End

The Beginning

I've never talked about this before. Honestly, I didn't believe that anyone would really listen to it, let alone believe it.

I was always a person who believed in God. I also believed in angels.

In fact, as a younger adult, I used to put angels around my home in many forms such as in photos and figurines.

I never went to church as a child.

I'd attended church only a handful of times in my life and usually because I was invited by a friend.

I remember attending a large church in Las Vegas after a fellow police sergeant was murdered.

He'd been shot in the head by a man in waiting. He'd been set up in an ambush.

His name was Henry.

I didn't know him very well, but his death had a profound impact on me.

I, along with thousands of others, attended Henry's funeral at a large Christian church in Las Vegas.

It was at Henry's service that I first heard the music of a band called "Mercy Me."

I found the piano to be so beautiful. The lyrics sang to my soul.

I remember a song called "I Can Only Imagine" streaming through the church and pictures of Henry's life on a movie screen for everyone to see in the various areas of the church.

There was one photo of Henry that I remember well.

It was one that looked like some sort of optical illusion.

He was photographed in the distance, with the appearance of the sun in his arms.

The photo looked like he was actually holding the sun.

I thought it was beautiful.

I listened to the music of "Mercy Me" and specifically the song "I Can Only Imagine" off and on for a couple of months after the funeral.

It was so full of hope and possibilities.

After some time passed, I went on with life and forgot about that song and its impact on me.

Many months later, I was driving alone in my car one day and listening to what was not considered to be a Christian and/or religious music station.

I had been going through some life things and had some tears in my eyes while I drove.

Well, that song came on.

I paused for a second, thinking, *Why is this song on? This isn't a Christian music channel.*

But then I let the words and the music envelop me, and I really started crying.

I mean, ugly crying. It was not pretty.

I was literally driving on the freeway like the hot-mess express.

At that time, I felt in my heart that I was meant to hear that song at that time, and well, I needed to hear it.

Sometimes we need to hear things.

I don't know why these memories have always stuck with me, but I know now that it led into what happened to me on the day of my emergency appendectomy surgery.

As the lights went out for me at the beginning of my surgery, I knew I was in trouble.

I could feel the poisons of the sepsis taking over my body, and I'd been…well, frightened I'd never see my family again.

After I was put to sleep, I started to be aware of something.

I could hear a female voice.

Now some of you may think "This lady is crazy for cocoa puffs" at this point. But hear me out. Stay with me.

I began hearing "Kasey. Kasey. Hello."

Had I been listening to too much Adele?

Possibly.

I remember the sound of the woman's voice growing louder. There was someone actually talking to me!

I know I know. Calm down.

The woman's voice continued to talk to me. She was trying to help me relax.

She said, "I know you are scared. It's going to be okay."

I kid you not.

She continued on with, "Kasey, I am your guardian angel."

I guess I was clearly confused. I wasn't sure what was happening.

I said back, "Well, if you are my guardian angel, then what is your name?"

I've always been a bit cynical. I mean, I call it "realistic," but you know, tomato-tamato.

Anyway, the female voice pressed on and said, "You have to give me a name."

Say what? I thought. "Don't angels come with names? Hadn't I heard of different archangels with names before? Wasn't there a movie out there with John Travolta in which he'd played the part of an Archangel Michael?"

She elaborated with, "I am you, and you are me. You have to give me a name."

What? I thought. "What do you mean, I am you and you are me?"

She then stated simply as if to end that part of the conversation, "I am you, and you are me."

Uhmmm…okay? I thought.

So because I'm fun like that, I thought about it for a bit.

I told the female voice claiming to be my "guardian angel" that I'd like to use the name Sarah. I'd always liked the sound of that name.

It had a soft, feminine, ethereal feel to it.

She immediately liked it too, and from that point on, she was known to me as Sarah.

Sarah and I began talking back and forth about her name.

Should she have a middle name?

What should her whole name be?

On and on. Back and forth we went.

No joke.

So I thought about it more. I'd always liked the Angel Store at the Lakes in Las Vegas. I'd seen these ceramic angel collections for sale in that store called Seraphim Angels.

They were absolutely beautiful.

I never collected them, but I'd always loved the name and the look of them.

So I suggested…or maybe she suggested? I don't really know.

Together, as a team, we came up with the name Sarah Femme.

Okay, I thought, still playing with the sound of her name.

I told her, "I will call you Sarah…Sarah Femme for Short."

She laughed at that.

She had the most wonderful sense of humor.

"Sarah…Sarah Femme for Short" began telling me, "It is not your time yet. You are going to be fine after the surgery."

(Looking back now, it took me a year for my stomach to be pain-free after that surgery, so I think the word *fine* is subjective. Don't get me wrong. I lived, and I'm grateful to have lived through it, but that recovery was no joke.)

Sarah, Sarah Femme for Short, further stated, "One day, you will write a book. I need you to write a book. There are some very important things I will tell you that I need for you to share with others."

Sarah, Sarah Femme for Short told me that I'd be in my recovery room soon, and she'd arranged for me to have a "private corner room."

She said she would send me some nice furry animals in my dreams so that I would not be alone when my husband had to leave the room to take care of other things.

Post-Appendectomy

I woke up in a hospital room of my own, sometime after surgery in the early afternoon hours.

I could hear machines beeping, and I felt so weak I could barely open my eyes.

Once I managed to open my eyes, I looked over to the right of my hospital bed and saw my husband staring at me.

He was literally bathed in the soft glow of the light coming through the window. His beautiful big blue eyes looked tired as he held my right hand from the side of the bed.

I can remember him just holding my hand and us both tearing up as we started to realize how close I'd been to leaving this earth.

I spent a week in the hospital after the surgery.

My back ached almost as much as my stomach did because of days of lying in bed before I even came into the hospital.

I struggled to get comfortable daily.

My husband was with me in the hospital most of the time, and my best friend flew across the ocean to be with me.

I think she'd known how close I'd been to leaving this earth as well.

When the nurses asked how my pain was on a zero-to-ten scale, I'd have to give them two numbers. One number for my back pain, and one number for my stomach pain.

I had a tube coming out of my stomach to drain the puss from the sepsis.

Several times a day, I was forced to blow air into an innocuous plastic contraption with a little ball. I was supposed to make the ball float.

That machine was not my friend.

I loathed it.

It was my nemesis.

My lungs worked throughout that week to float that stupid little ball, and every time I was forced to exercise my lungs, I thought I'd failed.

Every day, it seemed I'd have to have more blood drawn.

I'd been so dehydrated when I came into the hospital and after surgery that the nurses on my floor had to call a pediatric nurse with a special talent for poking needles into the tops of hands.

They did this out of mercy for me.

They'd tried and tried to find a vein and poked me so many times I felt like a "pin cushion."

I was relieved when they finally relented and called in backup.

I remember asking that nurse who was ultimately successful in inserting a "baby" needle in my left hand if it was difficult for her to work in the pediatric unit.

I will never ever forget her reply. She said, "Well, the highs are higher, but the lows are even lower."

On several occasions during that week in the hospital, I saw little woodland forest animals climbing on the walls of my hospital room. I saw "squirrels, foxes, and birds."

I recall people dressed in white coats coming into the room to ask me if I was having any issues with the pain medications I was on in recovery. They actually asked me if I was seeing things. I remember thinking, *Why are they asking me if this medicine is okay? Don't they know?*

At one point, I remember reporting to a lady who'd come into my room to inquire about the medications again that I'd been seeing little woodland-type animals on the wall.

I told her that I didn't mind seeing the animals because they were cute and seemed friendly.

I remember the woman saying something like, "Well, they are friendly now, but they can turn scary and frightening."

My pain medications were switched to something else after that.

All in all, I lost about twenty-five pounds that week on a "white" food "bland" diet of Jell-O and broth.

I remember just being so grateful to be strong enough to take my first shower in a room off the hallway of the hospital and even more grateful that I could go to the bathroom again on my own by the end of the week.

While I'd been in the hospital for that week, I'd learned that my dogs had a smelly encounter with a skunk, and the skunk won. While outside in our front yard, they'd been sprayed in their faces by a small skunk lurking in the rhubarb bush near the porch, and the dogs proceeded to run into the house, practically frothing at the mouth and drooling skunk-smell juice and drool from their jowls. The dogs apparently rubbed their dripping skunk-juice faces all over the carpet in the living room, trying to get the fowl spray and taste out of their mouths and off their bodies. My husband and best friend had done all that was possible in attempting to eliminate the smell from the dogs and the skunked carpet, but nothing seemed to work completely. There's an old remedy floating around about tomato juice working to eliminate skunk odor. It didn't. Dozens of cans of tomato juice later, and the smell still permeated the entire downstairs for weeks, and the dogs were bright pink. When I was released from the hospital and I arrived home with the assistance of my family, I was actually somewhat grateful I couldn't move very well and needed to rest in my bed upstairs. The smell of the skunk was still alive and well throughout the downstairs when I entered the house. It was enough to make me choke and gag. If I'd had much in my stomach at that point, it might have been lost. I was still so weak that I ended up needing bed rest for a couple weeks after I arrived home.

My husband brought me broth for that first week as I tried to gain my strength back.

It was an effort to even make it up and down the stairs of my home at that time. I had to stop midway up the stairs to catch my breath.

After another week or so, I started wandering out to the front porch for some sunlight, and even later, I began to walk around the yard to see how my flowers were doing.

I could not walk very far without being winded.

I remember the air was thick with smoke from the forest fires in the area, and I'd try not to be outside for too long inhaling it.

As my body healed over the next year and I regained my strength, my memories of Sarah faded in time.

In fact, I think I began to forget her visit entirely.

COVID-19

The Aftermath

As the course of three years post-COVID-19 took its toll on me and the "pressure canning" feeling in me really began to come to full steam around my fiftieth birthday, I began to think about writing a book.

I'd wanted it to be my "memoir" and a legacy for those I would leave behind.

I will admit here that January 2024 was one for the books in my life. I began the new year with this feeling that something was just…off.

I'd really let my use of my device become the most important thing in my life, and I felt this sense of guilt every day.

I'd become agitated with the lack of "humanity" I'd see flashing before my face, and I even started lashing out at people online who made thoughtless comments about other people. I'd known these people in "real life," and I'd respected them for decades.

I began writing stories for my memoir on January 11, 2024, as a way to just release some of my frustrations and tell my story.

I'd completed three or four stories about my memories and even sent some to my best friend to evaluate.

As soon as I'd sent her the drafts, I'd have second thoughts.

I'd felt they were too "edgy" and had a certain "rawness" that might put off anyone reading the material.

At some point, mid-January, I quickly became quite literally enveloped in an insomnia so unbelievable it's difficult to describe.

I found myself thinking of that old but awesome movie *Sleepless in Seattle*.

But I was just sleepless…in Montana.

The insomnia lasted about two and a half weeks total, but I do believe that there was one week in particular that I only was able to get about three hours of sleep.

I'd lay down, toss and turn, partially fall asleep, only to wake up again in an hour.

It went on and on like this.

I was also never able to take a nap during the day.

I'd struggled with napping during the day since I worked graveyard hours for the police department.

I began to simplify things in my life immediately.

I shut off my devices and closed out the online world, thinking it would help.

I cut caffeine, limited any unnecessary people contacts, set some boundaries, and just concentrated on my own personal rest.

Even though I wasn't sleeping at all, I tried to focus simply on making my bed every morning. This basic task made me feel better and gave me hope for what was to come in the evening for sleep.

Side note on beds: I love a well-made bed. If I only do one thing for the day, I am going to choose to make my bed. I am fortunate to have a warm soft bed and I've always believed my bedroom was my sanctuary. I wanted it to feel good.

I wanted it to look good.

I wanted to walk into my bedroom after a long day and say, "Hey, gorgeous, I've been waiting for you" to my bed.

I think, these thoughts about controlling "all the feels" of my bedroom came about after I worked in the Clark County Detention Center in Las Vegas (jail) for a year when I was eighteen to nineteen years old and after I experienced working in the streets of Downtown "Fremont Street" Las Vegas as a brand-new baby cop at the old age of twenty-one.

I saw a lot of despair and hopelessness in the eyes of the homeless in the Downtown Area.

They all had a story—drugs, alcohol, a broken heart, you name it.

For whatever reason, these people were never able to recover from life's hardships.

They were invisible.

Almost no one ever made eye contact with them.

They were cast aside.

They were inconveniences. They slept on the street, on bus stop benches, in alleys, and they didn't have beds.

I won't go into any more on that subject but my point is…everyone needs love.

And make your bed.

Sleepless Continued

At some point in all my constant tossing and turning at night in January, I began having some very intense dreams.

In my dreams, I began to hear a voice again.

Yes, yes, we've already covered this, but here she was again.

The voice sounded like that beautiful Adele song again. "Hello." You know the one.

Almost everyone has a face they picture when that song comes on.

I remember thinking, *Adele…that you?*

And just like that, Sarah, Sarah Femme for Short was back in my dreams, exchanging thoughts again.

(I'll just refer to her as Sarah for the rest of this book now that you know her full name.)

Sarah began to remind me that she needed me to write "that" book she'd told me about during my appendectomy surgery.

She said, "It's time. You must write the book."

I told her that I was writing a book and that it was going to be a memoir about my life.

But Sarah persisted.

I mean, she was unbelievably relentless in my dreams.

She even told me I would not be able to sleep until I began writing the book for "humanity."

She said I must share "her messages" and "His messages" and "their messages."

She would not stop.

Remember the Energizer Bunny? The bunny would keep going and going and going?

That was her.

The phrase "The beatings will continue until morale improves" comes to mind now as well.

"Humanity must hear these messages," she said. She was just so pushy.

She'd add, "People have lost their way. They need to come home."

At some point, early on in the "sleepless" week, she told me to start keeping notes in a book.

She started telling me, "Write this down. You will need it to write the book."

She repeated that over and over.

What could I do?

I wanted to just sleep, but Little Miss Pushy Pants would not stop coming at me.

I would tell her, "Leave me alone!"

And she would simply say no.

The Police Academy

Inspections and Uniforms

Sarah told me I needed to write things down when I woke, and she'd made a statement in my dreams about my never having to remember things like I "had to in the Police Academy."

She then flashed me a couple of pictures of moments from my Police Academy days in 1994.

The first scene she displayed in my dreams was the picture of what is called first inspection in law enforcement.

First inspection was an event in which all the new police recruits lined up in somewhat of a military formation and were examined and sometimes aggressively questioned by more seasoned and tenured police officers called TAC officers.

TAC officers made up what was known as the TAC staff at the academy.

TAC officers had uniforms that were impeccable.

Their uniforms were form-fitted and cut and sewn perfectly.

The leather on their police belts, shoes, and brim of their perfectly professional police hats practically sparkled in the morning sun.

The gold badges and gold name tags on their chests were so shiny they actually reflected the light as well.

Police inspections, especially at the beginning of the academy, were meant to simulate some of the situations new recruits would encounter once they graduated.

The inspections allowed the TAC officers to see how a new recruit might react under pressure.

It seemed that the less composed a new recruit was in inspection, the more the recruit would be singled out and given extra special attention by the TAC staff.

If any weakness was displayed, a new recruit would quickly become a professional at taking nonintentional spit in the face from one or several screaming TAC officers.

That recruit would also become adept at push-ups, running laps called grinders and writing something I recall as DRs (deficiency reports).

The flawless-looking TAC staff would march out of the training building and start yelling at recruits in the parking lot who were lined up in the hot desert sun, waiting to get the whole event over with and behind them.

I'd often hear the yelling start from the TAC officers as they'd barely exited the building and were almost a block away.

They'd move toward us as a team like a hungry pride of starving lions from out of view while we were to remain at the position of "attention," unable to move our eyes anywhere other than straight forward.

We were basically sitting there waiting to be devoured like injured zebras.

The whole debacle would be witnessed by what I'll call the Peanut Gallery.

The Peanut Gallery was usually made up of a band of newer police officers who'd recently experienced a successful transition from the Police Academy to the streets. They would show up, bring their hypothetical popcorn, and watch the comedy show.

Attending a first inspection after one graduated was a rite of passage for some.

They were just so relieved it wasn't them being inspected that it made the show all the more funnier to watch as the new recruits struggled with even basic directions under pressure.

The new recruit's uniform was a far cry from the "spit-shined law enforcement fashion plate" uniforms of the TAC officers.

Our drab beige uniforms were often baggy and made of cotton. They wrinkled easily, were too lightweight for the fabric to hang properly, and they just looked "dumpy and sloppy."

Our name tags consisted of an "index" card with our name printed out on it. The index card was inserted in a flat plastic cover with a sort of "safety pin" mechanism on the back of the plastic to affix it to our uniform shirts, centered above the right breast pocket.

The name tag was always flopping around and was almost never centered as it was supposed to be.

I think, in retrospect, it was always meant to be that way.

Recruits were not police officers yet, and the name tags and badges were to be earned.

There was a budget cost associated with a uniform, especially for a police department the size of Las Vegas Metro.

If a police recruit were to wash out of the academy, the extra dollars spent for a polished uniform and name tag would not be lost.

The real pièce de résistance of the entire police recruit uniform was the hat/cap.

While the TAC officers sported clean, crisp, official military-style caps with splashes of brass and patent leather shining in the sunlight, our hats were the exact opposite.

We were required to wear an extra-large and tall "crowned" and extra-large, wide-brimmed baseball cap while outside doing anything related to the academy in our goofy tan uniforms.

As I wrote this book and looked up the specific names for the different parts of the baseball cap to accurately describe it for you the reader, I laughed when I saw the word *crown*.

I thought, *Crown? Right! If I were a princess and I was presented with a crown like the one I suffered through in the Police Academy, I'd fire the designer thinking someone better fix this crown situation real quick.*

Even the most handsome police recruits in the academy had difficulty pulling off that monstrosity of a hat.

The whole police recruit uniform was designed to make the recruit have "all the feels" of being a first-class Deputy Doofy.

As the police recruits stood at the military position of "attention" in formation, the TAC officers began strutting around like elaborately decorated male peacocks, giving each recruit a chance to be in the dreaded limelight.

The inspection process seemed to take hours, and because of the heat in Las Vegas (an egg can literally be fried on the sidewalk at certain times of the day), our morning formations often required the visit of an ambulance because of a recruit passing out from the heat or coming close to it.

The actual process rarely deviated. The TAC officer would take a large step, do a "left face" (in my case), and I'd find myself nose to nose with intense eyes and my goofy hat brim being pushed back by the TAC officer's short and sporty patent leather hat brim.

Once the TAC officer stood nose to nose with the recruit, the TAC would begin firing questions at each recruit in a quick fashion while simultaneously inspecting their uniforms.

It was at this point and time in inspection that one's study habits and the ability to retain information came in quite handy.

The TAC officer would also inspect the recruit's weapon, almost assuredly finding old grease or a minuscule piece of dust in the crevices of the metal.

The TAC officer would then look the recruit over nice and slow-like, find a bug or a piece of dog hair on a uniform, and immediately crush the recruit with a verbal attack so bad you'd think the recruit made fun of the TAC's mother.

The TAC would fire off "400 Codes" (Police Codes) and words like "probable cause," "reasonable suspicion," and "burglary" into the face of the recruit.

The recruit would then be expected to spout what the "400 Code" meant and/or the definition for the police "terms" verbatim according to Nevada Revised Statutes (Nevada Law.)

I still remember vividly saying with assertion, "Sir! Burglary, sir! Every person who, either by day or night, enters any structure, with intent, to commit grand or petit larceny, any felony, assault or battery, is guilty of burglary, sir!"

(Note, this is from my memory. I have not looked up the Nevada Revised Statute to verify if the "burglary definition" is the same today as it was thirty years ago.)

(I once had a TAC officer ask me in the TAC office how I remembered my 400 Codes and "definitions" so well. I told him that it was just the way my mind thought. I told him that I'd often wake up in the middle of the night and see that it was "zero four… something" [military time like 0404, 0414, 0444] and my mind automatically thought of the code while I was barely awake. It wasn't something I made any effort to do. It just happened that way for me.)

The above first inspection description was the first picture and scene(s) Sarah flashed before me in my dreams, but I'll end this section on a little "nugget" I learned about uniforms from someone I admire very much.

The woman I admired very much was/is named Kathy.

She was a dedicated and committed, beautiful-petite force of nature, whom I'd met at eighteen years old while I worked as a police cadet at what was called Southwest Area Command in 1993.

Kathy ultimately retired at the rank of deputy chief, sometime in or around 2012. (The title of deputy chief was a very top position in the chain of command for Las Vegas Metro, and it was directly under the assistant sheriff in the organizational chart.)

Over the years, Kathy helped a lot of younger officers, sergeants, and lieutenants who had aspirations of promotion to higher ranks within the police department.

She was never compensated for it; she just did it because she cared.

Kathy took me "under her wing" almost immediately when I joined the police department, and she assisted me in my preparations for testing for the positions of police sergeant and police lieutenant.

I'd kept notes of all the tips and pointers she gave me in our meetings to help me prepare to stand above the crowd in the testing process and I'd labeled the notes "Sessions with Kathy."

I still remember most of what Kathy tried to instill in me, but one piece of advice stands out and is relevant to this section of this book.

Kathy once told me that people make a lot of "assumptions" about the way a "uniform should look" on a person.

She said that the police captains and lieutenants from other agencies who graded our promotional processes were no different.

She'd said that people will judge the way a "uniform looks" on someone without even thinking about it.

I'd later give her statements on "uniforms" real thought.

Along with the uniform inspections, we'd had some instruction in the academy on the topic of command presence in a uniform, but I didn't really give it more than superficial thought until Kathy said those words to me.

I was very young in the academy, and I didn't come from a military background.

I often thought that the Inspections were unnecessary for people like me.

Of course, I was going to put my best foot forward.

But I quickly understood that everyone has a different standard when it comes to putting their own best foot forward, and the whole reason there is an inspection process in a Police Academy is to ultimately ensure that a recruit has every tool they possibly can to stay alive in their careers.

Kathy put the importance of a "professional appearance" in a way I understood.

I knew that the "uniform appearance" was judged by not only promotional test graders and evaluators but by almost every single person I'd encountered in that uniform.

I began to understand that the way a person looked and carried themselves in a police uniform was often the first thing potentially dangerous people also looked at in sizing up whether they would cooperate or not cooperate with an officer's lawful instructions.

Kathy told me that our uniform was not created to fit the female body in a way that was very flattering.

With the bulky bulletproof vest, thirty pounds of gear, heavy wool pants, and "masculine" appearance, it was nearly impossible to not be "judged" in that uniform as a woman.

She suggested I wear a business suit to test for my promotions, and it was a suggestion I took to heart and never deviated from that point on.

The Police Academy Hostage

Barricade Practical Problem

The second and last Police Academy scene Sarah showed me in my dreams was that of a "quasipractical problem" I'd been selected to participate in sometime in my academy training.

A "practical problem" was something that was used to "test" a recruit's skills at handling the multitude of "policing situations" they may face on the street.

Up until Sarah showed me this scene, I hadn't thought about it since I was in the actual academy in 1994.

I was partnered with another female police recruit, and we'd stood outside the academy building in our Deputy Doofy uniforms.

Our TAC officer ensured our weapons were clear of any unintended ammunition, and we awaited the simulated details over the radio from our "pretend dispatcher" (also a TAC officer).

We were ultimately "pretend dispatched" to the "pretend call for help" from a local health and fitness workout facility (our police academy building.)

The details of the pretend call for service were as follows:

> TAC DISPATCHER. Two Academy Two copy a
> 416B
> (A 416B was an "other disturbance." It was a
> "catch-all code" for almost any call for ser-
> vice that didn't fit any of the other dozens of

400 Codes we were required to memorize in
the Academy.)

Me. Control, Two Academy Two, go ahead.

TAC dispatcher. Two Academy Two, be en
route to the *so-and-so gym* located at Mojave
and Washington Avenue. A male cus-
tomer is acting "irate" and causing a scene
inside the facility. Management wants him
"trespassed."

Me. Control, Two Academy Two. Copy that.
We'll be en route from Mojave and
Washington.

Me. Control, Two Academy Two. Arrived.

When my partner and I entered the "front door" to the pretend
gym, we immediately heard some loud yelling from where we stood
in the long hallway.

We each took what seemed like a split second to listen further
and evaluate what we were hearing taking place in the room off to
our right side (our academy classroom).

Suddenly, a man (TAC officer) clad in defensive tactics body
padding to include a face mask, burst through a set of doors leading
from the academy classroom into the hallway we were standing in.

He looked like that "Stay Puff" Marshmallow Guy from a com-
mercial in the 1980s, but his padding was black in color.

The Stay Puff Man also happened to have one of our other
female police recruits around the neck as she screamed "Help me!"
and feigned crying.

Stay Puff Man and the somewhat-hysterical-acting female
recruit advanced down the hallway towards the female locker room
away from our positions at the other end of the long hallway.

Looking back on this practical problem, I do believe the TAC
staff expected my partner and me to run down the long hallway after
the Stay Puff Man and pretend victim and straight into the locker
room behind them.

But we didn't.

We paused, not knowing if there might be another "pretend suspect" "lying in wait" for us to run past.

We thought there might be another suspect ready to jump out of the other various classrooms attached to the long hallway.

I remember thinking, *This is a setup. Another Stay Puff Man is going to take us out as we make our way down this long hallway.*

Another thing that caused me to pause for a half second regarding this particular practical problem was the fact that I'd already been exposed to police work in my duties as a police cadet on the streets for a whole year until I turned twenty and was eligible to attend the actual Police Academy.

I'd listened to a great deal of radio traffic between police officers and dispatchers by the time I was in that Academy, and I was somewhat familiar with how scenes like this would play out in the field.

With this knowledge, and thinking we now had what was referred to as a "hostage/barricade" in police language, my partner and I set up an immediate inner and outer perimeter, locked down the building, and began calling for all the "alphabet" response teams like medical, SWAT, and negotiators.

At some point about ten minutes into the practical problem, it must have become clear that we were not going to advance into what we felt was a trap.

Stay Puff Man and his female recruit hostage then emerged from the female locker room (along with a huge number of our fellow police recruits who were just observing the show).

The crowd moved down the hallway and stopped about thirty feet from our positions.

My partner and I had each taken cover in opposite doorway alcoves leading into classrooms but separated only by the open hallway.

My partner and I were essentially right next to each other but separated by that open hallway.

We used drywall as cover because it was the only thing available to us.

We each had our (empty) weapons drawn, and eyes and ears wide open, trying to evaluate the rapidly escalating and dynamic changes that were occurring with what had been just "other distur-bance" call a few minutes prior.

I remember the female recruit and her voice above all others the most.

She'd been screaming, fake crying, and essentially trying to cause us to get emotional I'd guessed.

She was yelling over and over, "Help me! Can't you see I'm in danger? Why won't you help me!"

She ranted on like that for at least a minute or two as the Stay Puff Man held his arm around her chest.

At some point, I thought I needed to clear my thoughts and well…just evaluate my next steps in the situation.

Her screaming was really getting on my nerves, and it was dif-ficult to think straight.

I calmly said at that point, "Hey, victim, why don't you shut up?"

I didn't mean it to be funny; in fact, I was stone-cold serious.

But there were several chuckles from the crowd of onlookers standing in the hallway anyway.

The practical problem was brought to an end by the TAC staff almost immediately after I made that statement to my fellow female recruit.

I remember thinking what an outstanding job she'd done of playing that victim role.

I'd later see that same victim behavior more times than I can count when I finally graduated from the academy and went to work on the streets of Las Vegas on my own.

The strange thing about this entire academy practical problem is this: I can remember almost all the general details of the pretend call for service.

But the one element and probably the most important detail of the whole event was the real or perceived presence of a weapon.

I cannot remember if there was an actual weapon being held to the female recruit's throat.

The memory is a very complex thing.

Sarah's Dream Harassment Continued

After Sarah flashed these memories from my academy days to me, she repeatedly told me to write down what she was saying. She was not asking me to do it. She was telling me to do it. She said I must write the book that she needed me to write. I was stubborn. I was confused. I was in a very blurry mental state because I hadn't really slept, and my mind wasn't getting the rest it needed to function properly. I was frustrated with her, and I was not cooperating like she wanted me to. But because I wasn't sleeping much at all and hadn't been for many days, I felt weak and a bit beat down. And when my stubborn obstinance at Sarah's intense and unrelenting instructions in my dreams to write down what she was saying and write the book she wanted me to write, I did the only thing I could do at that point.

I complied and began writing down everything she told me to write down.

I'd wake up after what felt like zero sleep and jot down all the notes I remembered.

We often argued in my dreams as well.

I told her I was writing a book and I told her to stop hijacking my book.

She laughed at that.

In fact, I wrote down in my book that she'd often giggled at me.

Sarah held her ground and began bringing reinforcements to my dreams.

She'd said she needed to bring reinforcements and backup because my human brain could not comprehend what she was telling me.

She started presenting me with voices and messages from my deceased loved ones and friends.

With each person I knew, I'd be presented with their voice and pictures from our moments together before they'd passed.

I'd hear their voices as if we were having the same conversations we'd had in the past.

Every single one of the people I'd known and loved came into my dreams to tell me they were all just fine.

They told me they "loved" me.

If I told them I loved them, they would all immediately repeat, "I love you" back to me.

If I told them, I "missed" them, each of them would state, "I know."

At some point, I remember daring them all to prove they were who they said they were and do Donkey impressions from *Shrek.*

From that point on, anything and everything I was told was in Eddie Murphy's famously recognizable voice but with Donkey's hilarious attitude.

For this next section, I'm going to start describing some of the people who visited me in my dreams, but I want to pause and offer this next piece of information from Sarah.

"Code Red"

The Most Important Part of This Book

If you don't read any further in this book, understand this: Sarah and I discussed Satan/Lucifer during her visits to my consciousness and dreams. She told me that the most important thing I must write in my book in the future would be the following:

"Don't ever refer to the evil one by his name. It gives him too much power."

You must tell everyone to refer to the evil one as Boof.

Giving him a funny name like Boof diminishes his power on a scale like none before.

"You must do this," she insisted.

So now instead of saying that phrase "Not today, Satan," you should always say, "Not today, Boof."

Sarah's "Backup"

I struggled with whether or not to put my visitors in this book or if I should leave them out altogether. In the end, I feel it is the right thing to do for the families and loved ones they left behind.

Ryan

Ryan was my brother-in-law. He was younger than I was, struggled with addictions, and didn't care for cakes or sweets at all our family get-togethers over the years he spent with us.

Ryan was imperfect, like all human beings, but he also had an incredibly loving and honorable side to him that one could see if they paid close attention to Ryan's actions.

On one occasion, Ryan made a promise to my son, his nephew. A lot of people say things and then don't ever live up to their words and promises, but not Ryan. Ryan promised my young son he would come over to play and spend some quality time with him. One day, he followed through and spent three hours with him. Ryan didn't have to do that, and I know he'd fit in the time around his own job and responsibilities. Technically, we weren't family or extended family any longer, but he did it anyway. I will never forget his display of integrity that warm afternoon and his desire to follow through with his promises with my young son.

Ryan's mom, Christine, has struggled like any mom would at the unbelievable loss of an adult child. Ryan asked me to share a song with her and tell her he knows she sees the messages he has sent. "Keep looking for the boats," he said. "Listen to Christina Perri's 'A Thousand Years,' Mom."

Tony

At some point, a former neighbor, coworker, and friend came to my dreams with Sarah.

I knew he'd died recently of cancer, and I also knew his wife had been struggling to deal with the loss of her longtime husband and father to her two beautiful, amazing children.

Tony told me that he'd been sending messages and signs to his wife in Las Vegas, and he wanted her to know that he knew—that she knew—all the messages were from him. He also told me to tell his sweet wife that she needed to listen to Michael Bublé's song "Lost."

Cliff

I'd met Cliff while working in the jail in Las Vegas, also known as the Clark County Detention Center.

He was a corrections officer at the time, and we became friends.

He was a very large black man with a quiet demeanor.

When I say large, I mean he was big-boned.

He wasn't overweight at all. It's just that his limbs, and the core of his body were just bigger than most people.

He was muscled, but his muscle was on the thicker side.

He was tall. I'm guessing six feet four, maybe six feet five?

He was hilarious but didn't often show it to most people.

Cliff was a Steelers fan.

He loved to bake, and he once brought me the best piece of carrot cake I've ever had.

Cliff was also a "tell it like it is" kind of person. He wasn't a game player.

Cliff was genuine and a dear friend for many years.

Cliff also visited me with Sarah.

He told me that he'd had some heart problems and died because his heart had not been able to handle the size of his body.

He left it at that.

During Cliff's visit with Sarah in my dreams, he told me, "You still need a sandwich."

He made me laugh in my dreams!

He'd flashed me a picture of me walking through a police station in Las Vegas called Hargrove at the time.

I'd been wearing a white tank top and dark navy blue capri pants as I moved my boxes in.

I'd been moving into my new desk and locker as I'd just been promoted to police sergeant in 2002 in what was called the William/Union (Sector Beats) area on the graveyard shift.

He flashed me the picture of him walking by me and quietly but sarcastically, saying, "You know you need a sandwich, right?"

I'd taken his statement to mean I could afford to put on a few pounds.

I'd been shocked to learn of Cliff's passing online sometime in 2020.

It saddened me to think he had never been married that I knew of and he'd left too soon.

During his visit in my dreams, he told me how he really felt about me. He said he'd never had the courage to express his true feelings to me and he regretted that.

He told me to listen to two songs and think of him.

The first song was by Jagged Edge called "Let's Get Married."

The second song was a song by Vanessa Carlton called "A Thousand Miles."

Cliff told me that I must do one thing when I listen to Vanessa Carlton's song.

I said, "What is that?"

He said, "You must pretend that I am Terry Crews from that movie *White Chicks* and that I'm singing to you in a convertible."

He made me laugh in my dreams again.

I wish people had known how funny Cliff was when he was here with us.

And lastly, regarding that carrot cake I mentioned above, I must be transparent when I tell you he asked me to say that he'd made the best carrot cake that I've ever had.

Larry

Larry was a man I had the most complete and profound respect for.

I first saw him in front of our class of 2/94 Police Academy, giving the class instruction on Special Weapons and Tactics, also known as SWAT.

His voice was deep and boomed across the room without much effort.

He'd had an absolute gift for articulating his thoughts.

He was also a fairly large muscled man with fair skin and brown hair.

He'd been a police officer in SWAT at the time he'd provided instruction to our Police Academy class, but I took one look at him when I was only twenty years old, and I knew he was going to do great things.

I knew he was a true leader.

His integrity was unmatched, and I could see that in the way he spoke and the way he'd carried himself.

I'd later have the opportunity to work with him when I worked directly for the Clark County Sheriff as a police sergeant in the sheriff's office located on the tenth floor of the city hall.

During my time in the sheriff's office, I remember Larry sitting down in a chair in front of my desk, and he was talking about one of his daughters and the man she'd been thinking about.

He'd been talking about what a man needed to be and how they needed to behave as men.

I believe Larry told me he was a bishop in the LDS Church sometime in that office or perhaps I was told that by someone else in the police department?

Larry always spoke with such clarity and humbleness, and I was so fortunate to have been able to share some moments with him while he was here.

He'd often make statements about "the human condition," and when I left the sheriff's office to work in the Sex Offender

Apprehension Program (SOAP), I often used that exact phrase because of him.

In fact, I still use it to this day.

Larry unexpectedly died sometime around 2015.

I remember being completely heart broken when I found out the news online.

It seemed every time I looked online, another great human was gone.

I think I'd placed him on a pedestal from the age of twenty, and his death really saddened me beyond words.

Over the past ten years since I retired, but increasingly so after Larry died, I'd see the number 4:44 on the clock almost every afternoon and every early morning when I woke up for whatever reason while sleeping.

It happened so often that I'd note it in my head and smile.

I always had this feeling that I was supposed to see those numbers.

The number 444 is significant to me and anyone who worked for the Las Vegas Metropolitan Police Department.

The number 444 is the four hundred code all the officers and dispatchers use to mean "Officer needs help. Emergency."

The number 444 is the real deal in my history and memory.

It always will be.

I have memories of friends and colleagues saying their call signs and yelling a breathless "444!" over their police radios when they were in trouble and they knew it.

Whenever I heard a 444 code over my police radio, it sent shivers up my spine.

With that particular code, the dispatcher would begin what is called a code red on the channel.

A code red meant "Emergency Exists. Emergency [Radio] Traffic Only."

With a 444 and code red in effect on any radio channel, anyone and everyone who could go to the 444 officer's aid was going.

There was often no radio traffic indicating other officers were on their way to provide backup. Everyone just knew they were on their way.

During the course of the intense insomnia week(s). I must have seen the number 4:44 on my clock five to eight times, but I wasn't keeping track.

During the course of the insomnia one afternoon in late January, I'd sat on my bed trying to type some of the thoughts out for the book that Sarah told me I had to write.

Determined to get some sleep that night, I'd been there on my bed for several hours at that point typing away.

Several things happened simultaneously as I sat on my bed, and I'm only going to share this because Sarah said I should in my dreams later.

As I typed on my bed, I looked up at the clock and saw it was 4:44 p.m.

I noted the numbers mentally.

Soon after I saw the time of 4:44 and noted it, I also received a message on my device from someone I did not know who told me that they were "thinking about me."

On the heels of that message on my device, my almost three-year-old male chocolate Labrador retriever ran upstairs and straight into my bedroom.

My Lab began whining next to my bed while looking up in the air.

He whined and shifted his body weight around nervously for about a minute, looking up into the air near my bed.

My dog was going absolutely crazy and moving around while whimpering and whining.

I moved to a plush chair in my room and called him to try to calm him down.

He kept looking up into the air all around me and jumping up as if trying to get at something.

He literally seemed scared and wanted to attack something for about thirty seconds to one minute more.

I then took my dog downstairs and was able to soothe him and calm him down.

Later that night in my dreams, Sarah brought Larry to my consciousness.

Larry told me that he'd shown me the number 4:44 over the past few years, and that night, he'd been trying to warn me with the clock numbers at 4:44 as I sat on my bed, typing Sarah's book.

He said he knew I would notice the number 4:44, and I'd pause.

He said that Boof was trying to intervene in my writing this book, and it was good I ultimately ignored the sudden message from the stranger on my device.

As I spoke with Sarah and Larry in my sleep, he also flashed in my head moments in time that he and I had worked together while I was a police sergeant in patrol while he was commanding SWAT and worked on the Crisis Negotiation Team.

Looking back on this event now as I am writing this book, I am not surprised by Larry's heroism.

Anyone who was fortunate enough to know him when he was alive knew he was a real-life hero and true leader.

To give you just a glimpse of the kind of amazing human he was, I'll share another story with you and I hope I am giving the impact of his statements justice.

One time, in another educational class Larry taught in one of my promotional training courses he'd made a statement about hostage negotiations.

He'd said something like, "When there are hostages there is no time for negotiations…how long would you like the police to wait to go into a hostage/barricade situation if it were your family being held hostage?"

During Larry's visit to me with Sarah he told me that he has a message and a few songs that he wants the men to listen to. He said that anyone who knew him would know the words were from him.

He said simply, "Take care of the women and children," and then gave me four songs for the men.

The first song was "It's Different for Girls" by Dierks Bentley.

The second song was "Better Man" by Little Big Town. Larry added, "She will miss you."

The third song was Keith Urban's "Female."

The last song was John Mayer's "Daughters."

For Larry's family, Larry told me to tell them, "I want them to KNOW that I love them."

Dana

Dana was someone I worked with in patrol in the northwestern part of Las Vegas for a brief period.

The man had a smile every time I'd seen him. He practically gleamed. He was such a happy person.

He was probably the most genuinely nice person I've ever met in my life.

He was soft-spoken, funny, had the hugest heart, and he was a Minnesota Vikings fan.

One time after I'd retired, I flew back to Las Vegas to handle some of my grandmother's affairs before moving her to Montana with me.

Dana picked me up from the baggage check at the airport, loaded my luggage into his patrol car, and drove me to the rental car place a few miles away.

When we went to say goodbye, he gave me a hug, and we took a selfie together.

He gave me a peck on my cheek at the last minute as we took a selfie, and I'd been shocked.

I told him, "Please don't do that."

I was married and had this ridiculous fear of that photo getting back to my husband and what he might think.

We took a few more selfies, and I ultimately said goodbye to Dana at the rental car place in what turned out to be the last time I ever saw him in person.

He'd send me some Police related poems online and then one day he just stopped sending things.

I learned near the Fourth of July in 2022 that he'd passed away because of cancer.

I was in Kalispel Montana about to go to the lake for the Fourth of July when I read the news.

I sat there at breakfast with my family so completely sad.

I hadn't even known he was sick.

And now he was gone.

After Dana passed, I'd often kick myself for behaving the way I did when he kissed my cheek with a peck during our selfie together.

That was just Dana being Dana.

He was so full of joy all the time, and all he'd been trying to do was show me he was happy I was visiting as it had been years since I'd seen him in person at that point.

Sarah brought Dana to my dreams, and he wanted his family to know he was okay. He also said, "Please tell them I love them and tell them to listen to a song by Pharrell Williams called 'Happy.'"

Melanie

Melanie was a friend.

She died around January 2023.

I remember getting a call one evening from another dear friend who still lived in Las Vegas.

Melanie was a mom, a wife, a sister, a daughter, and she also happened to be a district court judge in Las Vegas.

She was really stunning to look at.

She had long blond hair, dark-rimmed glasses, and kept her body very fit.

I first saw her in the courtroom wearing her dark-framed glasses, black judge's robe, and red lipstick.

I watched how she handled the cases in front of her, and I immediately liked her and wanted to know her.

I'd had in my mind at that time (2008/2009) that I'd wanted to retire from the police department and pursue a career as an attorney.

I knew Melanie's friendly and soft-spoken husband through my work, and so I set out to meet her through him.

One day, we arranged to meet at her office (judges' chambers) and walk across the street to the Golden Nugget Hotel and Casino for lunch.

Her office was beautiful with glorious sunshine streaming through the windows.

I remember her office furniture being heavy-looking with dark wood stain.

She'd had a large photograph in her office of John F. Kennedy in his presidential office with his two young children under his desk. I loved the "sweetness" captured in that photo of a man with his children underfoot.

But what really struck me in Melanie's office were the other photos—a glimpse of what I was to learn about Melanie's personality.

Her judge's chambers was an ode to the singer Pink.

She'd hung multiple large framed posters of Pink on the different walls of her office, and I soon learned that she was a very rock-and-roll-type lady.

She loved hot rods, chrome, the band Five Finger Death Punch, and egg-white omelets.

As we began to form a friendship over the next couple of years, I'd seen glimpses of Mel that I thought were somewhat troubled.

She had this very intense strength about her on the outside, but I remember asking her if she was "sad" while we waited for her car (A "tricked out" chromed and lifted white Chevy Tahoe, I believe?) at the Cosmopolitan Hotel and Casino one evening after a charity event for women and children victims of domestic violence.

She wasn't shocked that I asked her about her sadness at all.

She'd simply said that she was "sad" sometimes.

Her car was delivered by the valet attendant, and she drove off shortly thereafter.

After I'd learned of Mel's death last year (2023), I thought of her as I drove down the highway to attend my second Beekeeping 101 class.

I'd blasted Pink's music in my car so loud and sang the lyrics at the top of my lungs.

I had tears in my eyes at the unbelievable loss of her life.

I was so upset and thinking about her family and her children.

At one point, I actually had the thought that I needed to call my dear grandmother and tell her that Melanie was gone.

But then, I remembered.

I remembered that my grandmother had also been gone for three years at that point.

I couldn't call her anymore.

While I was sleepless, Sarah also brought reinforcements in the form of Melanie.

Melanie told me, "Thank you for being a friend to me."

She also told me some things she said I didn't need to share, so I am honoring her wishes.

At one point, as Melanie visited me in my dreams, she said she had a "message for the singer Pink."

I said, "What do you want me to tell her?"

She said, "Tell her I love her!"

I replied with, "Are you sure, Mel?"

Melanie had quite a way with words, and she replied with an expletive "F—— yeah!" When she said, "F—— yeah!" she also flashed me a picture of her holding up her arms and hands as if she was at a rock concert. The hand sign is known by many names to include "hang loose" or "rock on."

(The hand sign consisted of the index and pinky fingers extended straight up into the air while the middle, ring, and thumb fingers were curled toward her palms.)

Melanie told me that she wanted me to tell her family to listen to a song as well. She said the singer India Arie was not her usual style, but she asked that they listen to India's song called "This Too Shall Pass."

She said further, "They need to know it's not their fault."

I asked her if she wanted me to say anything else in particular in the book, and she replied, "I miss my kids."

She ended our conversation with, "You're an awesome singer."

My family

I was also visited many times in my dreams by all the members of my family. My mom and dad, my grandfather, and even my great-great-grandfather Charles Matthews also known as Billy Smith.

Mom, Karen

My mom and I never had much of a relationship. I always felt that our roles had been reversed, and I was the mom while she was the child. I always carried a lot of resentment and anger about our reversed roles.

She'd had a kind heart but she also had very serious addiction problems.

My mom visited me in my dreams with Sarah as well.

She told me, "I'm sorry I wasn't the mom you needed. Please forgive me. Please have mercy on me."

She asked me to listen to Meghan Trainor's song called "Mom."

She said, "Please picture me as 'that' mom, the one Meghan Trainor sings about."

"I'm so sorry."

Jack Edward Matthews

When Sarah brought my grandfather forward to talk to me in my dreams, he called me "baby" like he used to when I was a kid.

He told me that he knew that I knew it was him who visited me in my dreams in the year 2006.

I remember a dream I had in that year so vividly because I told my grandmother about it the following day on the phone while I was on a break at work in my duties as a police sergeant on the day shift in the southwest part of Las Vegas.

I told my grandmother that I'd had a dream about Granddad, and it was so clear.

I explained the dream to her like this, "I walked out to my backyard, and Granddad was there at dawn. There was soft lighting all around the landscaping and swimming pool, and he'd been sitting on a couch in the grass. He got up from the couch when he saw me come into the backyard, and he walked over to me. I asked him, "Grandad, is that you?"

He responded with no words. He simply cupped the cheeks of my face in both hands and looked into my eyes, smiling.

Grandmother, dragonfly

My grandmother is the last person I will write about, and she is the most challenging for me to write about.

We were both very strong-minded ladies, and from my teenage years forward, we sometimes struggled to see each other clearly.

She essentially became my mother when she thought she'd already raised her two children and was free from the responsibilities of parenting any longer.

Despite our various conflicts over the years, we were as close as any grandmother and granddaughter (mother and daughter) could be.

When my grandmother was dying in hospice in 2020, I sat next to her, held her hand, and asked her to show me dragonflies to show me she was near after she passed on to heaven.

She'd often worn brooches and pins of dragonflies, and I'd grown to love them as well.

While she was in hospice, I sat next to her and played some beautiful piano music for her to hear. She was not verbal and was in a coma-type state. She just appeared to be soundly sleeping.

The music I played for my grandmother was the soft piano music of the artist and pianist, Paul Cardell.

I'd first heard the music of Paul Cardell through my best friend's family. They'd often listened to it on Sundays.

The funeral for my grandmother came and went and my best friend insisted we go on a trip to Costa Rica to regroup and just get away for a bit. I didn't fight it.

On the last day of our trip, I didn't want to get out of the warm luxurious feeling waters of the lagoon-style pool at the resort we were staying at.

My bestie went to the tiki-hut-style bar and brought me back this little frozen adult beverage called the dirty monkey and placed it near the side of the pool edge where I'd perched myself in the sun.

My body was inside the pool as I leaned my head down onto the pavement of the cement outside the pool.

I had a large black sun hat on and rested my head on my folded arms basking in the sun.

At that moment, as I let myself think of my grandmother, I began missing her so much. I was surrounded by what seemed like a hundred gold-colored dragonflies.

In fact, as I continued to lie my head down on the pavement of the pool decking, one large gold-colored dragonfly landed on my finger where it stayed for several minutes.

(Golden yellow was my grandmother's favorite color. She never deviated from her love of the golden yellow.)

My bestie snapped a picture of my special visit from the golden dragonfly, and it is a memory I will always have of a visit from my grandmother.

I returned from Costa Rica in February 2020.

I began handling the various tasks involved with settling my grandmother's estate.

While I was handling my grandmother's last wishes and continuing through the last four years after her death, I'd often listen to music on a small selection of stations I preferred.

These were also not stations I'd ever expect to hear the music of Paul Cardell.

On many occasions over the past four years, I'd unexpectedly hear the keys of his piano filling my ears and every single time I teared up in thoughts of my grandmother dying in hospice.

Dreams of grandmother, dragonfly

Right after my grandmother passed, my brother and I began planning her funeral. She hadn't wanted a big to-do after her death. When she passed in Montana with me, I was torn about a funeral for her. She'd had many dear and cherished friends in Las Vegas, people that she'd known and loved and who'd loved her for decades. She'd had business contacts that she'd known since the seventies through my grandfather's very large, statewide real estate business, and she was someone who was so memorable to many people. She was an educated, accomplished, and classy lady with a brilliant mind. She had this ability to make a big impression on people. I'd always joked that you'd never know she was a shorter lady and not six feet tall herself due to the confidence and strength she effortlessly displayed.

Knowing all this about my amazing grandmother, I set out to make her funeral in Las Vegas, bigger than she'd probably like. I ordered dozens of yellow roses and dozens of fancy baked goods with coffee and tea to be served after the short goodbye to her from her friends and loved ones.

One night, very shortly after she died and before her funeral, she came to me as I slept. Her voice and words told me that she was not happy with me. I never saw her in a dream, but her voice, very vividly, told me, "Kasey, stop it with the big plans for the funeral. Just stop it. You don't need to do anything more."

I had several dreams of my grandmother within a couple of months of my return from Costa Rica. I remember them so clearly because I dictated everything I could remember of them right after I woke up.

The first dream was on April 21, 2020, and it went like this,

> I had this dream between 4:00 a.m. and 6:00 a.m. I remember looking at the clock before falling asleep again right before 4:00 a.m., and I woke up just after 6:00 a.m.
>
> I had this dream that I looked outside, and it was very green in my backyard.
>
> I could see really large red apples under my apple tree.
>
> I walked outside to take a closer look and a whitish/gray shaggy-haired little dog appeared wagging its tail.
>
> The dog then dove under the grass and the grass looked watery.
>
> Another little shaggy dog appeared and also dove under the "watery" grass.
>
> Then as if I was being lifted flat on my back straight into the clouds, my body was straight and I began floating very gently toward the clouds.
>
> I was not scared at all.
>
> Once my body reached the "big white fluffy" clouds, I saw grandmother sitting on something white.
>
> It looked like a surfboard.
>
> It looked like grandmother was straddling a white surfboard floating in the clouds.
>
> She sat on the surfboard facing another woman who was also straddling the white surfboard.
>
> The two ladies were facing each other while straddling a surfboard!

I was off to the side of the surfboard… floating.

The lady who faced my grandmother on the surfboard was in her twenties with blonde shoulder-length hair.

My grandmother was a little younger than she was when she died.

I guessed seventy-five or so, and she was wearing a pink-and-white checkered Miss Elaine nightgown that she'd used to love from Dillard's.

Grandmother told me to stop worrying about her.

She said that she was happy with this nice woman from New Jersey.

The blonde girl from New Jersey began talking nonstop.

I mean, she was talking so fast and so much. She would literally not be quiet.

I was trying to listen to what my grandmother was saying as she sat on the surfboard, but the Jersey Girl insisted on talking over her.

I finally looked at Jersey Girl and said, "Shut your mouth. I'm trying to listen to my grandmother."

And instantly, she stopped talking.

I told my grandmother that I missed her and I loved her.

I put my hand on her hand and felt her hands touching mine.

I felt her hands the way they used to feel.

She cupped my hand with her other hand. I woke up with this intense feeling of gratitude, and I felt that she was okay and happy.

The second dream was on April 28, 2020. I dictated the following.

> So last night's dream went as follows. I unlock Grandmother's door to her house. I prepare to enter, and I open the door. Grandmother is there in her house, shuffling about like she had in her later years but fifteen to twenty years younger. She is unpacking boxes and busy doing something inside a cardboard box.
>
> The light from the sun is shining through her bedroom window, on the lightly stained wood floor, and the window lighting is lighting her up as she stands near the kitchen, between the dining room and the kitchen.
>
> She is wearing one of her multicolored—primarily purple-and-mauve—striped T-shirts with coordinating button-fly canvas-type shorts.
>
> I look at her in disbelief and start crying because she's not supposed to be there; she died. And I tell her, "Grandmother, you aren't supposed to be here. You died. I am the one who is cleaning up your place. I am taking care of it."
>
> Everything goes dark in my dream at that point, and then I wake up in the dream to a cat purring in my face and licking my forearms to wake me up while I'm still asleep but dreaming.

Interestingly, for approximately the first two weeks after my grandmother died in late January 2020, I was taking care of her two beloved cats in her home. Every day, I would go over to feed them and take care of their litter box. I had done some of my grandmother's laundry and left some towels and washcloths folded in neat piles on her bed for about a week and a half. The towels and washcloths were of various colors except for five or so washcloths that were all simply bright yellow.

For a week and a half, every day that I'd arrive to my grandmother's house, I found only the bright-yellow washcloths on the floor in front of the bed. I'd fold them again and leave them placed neatly in a folded pile on her bed.

I'd figured it was one of her cats that knocked them off the folded piles on the bed, but still…I'd felt this strangely happy anticipation every time I arrived at her home. I'd drop my keys and bag in her kitchen on the counter, then walk straight to her bedroom to check out the yellow-washcloth situation.

There were many other washcloths and hand towels of different colors folded on the bed, some in the same pile as the yellow ones, but the bright-yellow washcloths were the only linens to ever be displaced daily onto the floor.

It became a small phenomenon I looked forward to with every visit. I explained what I encountered with the yellow washcloths to my husband, and he began to see it too during our visits to take care of her cats. I talked about it to my best friend and sent her a video of one of my arrivals to the house and my finding them on the floor one day. It was an amazing feeling all produced by what seemed like coincidence, but the simple little yellow squares of fabric on the floor felt deliberate—almost as if…my grandmother was sending messages to me using her cat and favorite-color washcloths.

Another dream I had between 2020 and 2023 was not nearly as clear and very quick.

In fact, I didn't even take any notes on it, but I still remember it.

My grandmother came to me in a dream excited to tell me that she'd just gotten "married."

The picture of a white-haired, smiling shorter man came to my dream.

That was it, and then it was over.

During my sleepless week(s), Sarah brought my grandmother with her on many occasions.

We had many discussions, and we forgave each other for some of the issues we'd had.

We told each other "I love you."

My grandmother shared with me that she'd heard the music I'd played for her while she was dying in hospice and she'd thought it was the most beautiful piano she'd ever heard.

We continued to have conversations on her visits with Sarah, and most of those conversations will just stay with me, but she did ask me to talk about one significant thing that occurred during the sleepless week(s).

Do you remember that story I told you about the district attorney's office and my meeting with the man who prosecuted my father for "arson?"

(He said my father "maintained he'd burned that house down because [my uncle] his brother-in-law had been molesting his [Jon's] child [me]?")

Well, over the years growing up, my uncle would come to our house, and I'd be forced to share holidays and holiday meals with him.

When my father got out of prison, he'd often be forced to sit at the same table with my abusive uncle just so he could see me and spend some time with me.

My grandparents never fully understood what happened to me, and they could never see the pictures in my mind of the condominium where the abuse took place and the white door with the brass locks.

A four-door white sedan with two men in it just showed up at my elementary school one day, and I was called out of my second-grade class (Mrs. Hicks) without any explanation at all.

I spent what felt like the whole month leading up to and through Christmas in a place called Child Haven.

I'd received one or two sessions of counseling as a young girl afterward, but I'd always been seen as the "little adult," so no one thought what happened to me was any big deal.

After my grandmother died, I became responsible for that very condominium I'd pictured that day in the district attorney's offices.

The same condominium where I was sexually abused.

Per my grandmother's instructions after her death, I was to allow my (slightly slow) "uncle" to continue living in the condominium that I was supposed to maintain for him.

I was to preserve the condominium so that it could be passed on to another family member.

After 2020, I wrestled and agonized over having to take care of a condominium for an abusive uncle.

How could my grandmother do this? I thought.

The uncle died in the winter of 2021 and the condominium sat empty for a large period *of time.*

I did not have the ability to sell the condominium on my own without permission from the court because of some legalities and other people involved.

Squatters broke in and caused a significant amount of costly damage to the inside of the condominium in June/July 2023, and I decided I wanted to be finished with taking care of the condominium for good.

I hired an attorney to petition the court so that I could then sell the property.

I was denied.

When my attorney reported back that the court denied my ability to sell the property, I was done.

I told my attorney that I wanted to relinquish any responsibilities I had for the property and move on.

This process to relinquish my responsibilities started on September/October 2023.

In January, toward the end of my sleepless week(s), I began writing this book.

I'd started to sleep a little better, and Sarah was finally off my back and mostly out of my dreams.

I sat on my couch pounding away at the keyboard. My head was full of words I needed to type when I got a phone call.

My attorney's office called and told me that as of that very minute I was no longer responsible for the condominium and that the responsibility for the property would be handled by the state.

I breathed a sigh of relief at the phone call. Tears formed in my eyes, and I just began typing again.

Diamonds and stars

After Sarah brought all her backup in the form of my deceased family and friends to try to persuade me to write this book, she told me I should listen to a song about my friends and family members when I woke. The song was "Diamonds" by Rihanna.

Moving On

Looking back, as I completed this book, and even after Sarah presented all my loved ones and friends to me, I argued with her.

I didn't understand what was happening, and I was frustrated with her telling me all the time that I didn't understand because my "human brain" could not grasp something like this.

I began asking questions. I asked a lot of questions.

I asked questions like a four-year-old asks questions.

It went something like this:

> "Why do I have to write the book?"
> "Because you are strong."
> "Why do I have to write the book?"
> "Because you are chosen."
> "Why am I chosen to write a book?"
> "Because you can write."

We must have bantered back and forth with these same three questions hundreds of times.

I really could not believe what I was being told.

When I awoke from the dreams, I'd always write what she told me and reflect.

Her statement to me, "Because you can write," caused me to reflect on what others said to me about my ability to put words on the page over the years.

My high school chemistry teacher told me that I could and "should" write.

I wrote an essay in competition with hundreds of other high school seniors after my "Career Day-Ride Along" with a recruiter from the police department when I was seventeen. I'd won first place and $1,000.

Many of my supervisors at the police department often mentioned my writing to me up to and including the sheriff who ran the entire agency.

As I began writing this book, I wondered if I was always meant to write this book. In my dreams and consciousness, Sarah confirmed this was true. She said I was always meant to write this book. It was destined from my birth. She stated this to me dozens of times. She repeated statements to me over and over until I understood and remembered them. She made many of the same statements hundreds of times as I struggled to understand what was happening in my mind.

Sarah was always very patient with me, but she was assertive when she needed to be.

She always spoke in a kind, soft voice.

She told me that it was okay to keep asking the same questions, and she patiently kept answering every question I presented to her.

I never saw an actual image or figure of anyone in my (for lack of a better term) dreams.

At one point, I remember asking Sarah if God was there.

He immediately said, "Yes, I am here."

I said, "I can't see you?"

He said, "Tell me what you want me to look like."

I told him I pictured him looking like a thinner Santa Claus with long white hair and a crown wearing a long flowing white robe.

He showed himself to me in my mind as that very picture.

He looked majestic and strong but also kind and smiling.

In our conversations, Sarah had some vocabulary that she used with me over and over.

At times, we'd have difficulty communicating and if I asked a question she didn't want to answer or perhaps couldn't, she would just go silent.

At times, if I phrased the question another way she would then be able to answer me.

Sarah's responses to my questions were often met with the following phrases, which she instructed me to write down so I did:

"I know."

"He loves you."

"Yes."

"No."

"Thank you."

"You're welcome."

"It's okay."

"Maybe."

"Free will."

"Have no fear."

"You are safe."

"Yep." (She was trying to be funny here. She said "yep" often.)

"You know the answer."

"I'll tell you later."

"You'll find out."

"You will know."

"It's a gift."

"You are me and I am you."

"Don't think too much."

"Let it happen."

"You're not in control." (Not going to lie, she said this one hundreds of times.)

"Human brain."

"They have their own path."

"It happens when it's supposed to happen."

"Calm yourself. There is no need to fear."

"You must be selfless in this."

"Bubble." (Bubble was interesting. Sarah told me to imagine a bubble around me if I thought about anything negative. She'd said to say the word *bubble* in my head and imagine anything negative I encountered when I woke up, bouncing off my bubble.)

"Recalibrating." (Sarah said this term to me many times in our dream discussions. She said that Santa Claus and the angels will often have to recalibrate after people use their own free will and start traveling down a path that isn't meant for them.)

"Overachiever." (Yes, she called me this term several times. Those who know me well will understand.)

At one point, I remember asking her, "Do you always say what's on your mind or is it just my lucky day?" She giggled. "Yep."

She'd laughed when I nicknamed her "Wrecking Ball" after Miley Cyrus's song. She'd thought it was hilarious. I, however, was not laughing. I was serious. I just wanted to get a few hours of sleep.

Some of the terms that she used, but not often were these.

"You have not failed until you've stopped trying."

The phrase "Are you mad-mad?" (Sarah would use this phrase to try to make me laugh when I told her to leave me alone so I could just get some sleep.)

At one point, I asked Sarah, "What if I refuse?"

There was no answer. I was presented with silence.

"There are no time limitations."

"Spread the word. Help the people. Tell people there's a lot of darkness that tries to hold back the knowledge and awareness of this place."

"God wants us to be aware that death is not the end. It is not the finality we've been led to believe."

"Look for the numbers 11:11 on the clock. Any form of 11 is an angel number."

"Post only the good. It weakens him [Boof]."

"Make phone calls more."

"Send messages less."

"Listen to your inner voice, especially between the hours of 3:00 to 5:00 a.m." ("Preserve your ideas from those hours.")

"There is a profound ability of the subconscious to shape our reality."

"Early morning clarity is more than coincidental."

"Get curious, brave girl."

"This story will be heard by many at what feels like a dark time."

"There are forces trying to hide us."

"I've always been here."

"Guilt is not from us."

"The people need to have hope."

"You don't have to be anywhere specific to pray. Just pray."

"Call Him. He hears you."

"When you are scared and on your knees, you must ask Him to help you."

"You must ask for forgiveness."

"It's okay to…but you are more powerful if you love."

"Things do not matter. They should go if you don't need them. Let go of them."

"Be gentle with children in the morning. Take five minutes. Whisper in the early morning with them. Cuddle."

"Take time to be gentle with children at bedtimes."

"Ask children about their day at school. Ask them to tell you about their day. Listen."

"Pray over children."

"Pray with children."

"He hears you."

"He can hear you."

"Be gentle with spouses."

"Numbers are significant."

"You must ask."

"Small thoughts small minds, their path is different."

"Parenting is the most thankless job."

"Choose your words carefully."

"There is power in this, the ultimate influencer."

"You are the Wi-Fi."

"I have moved your feet and moved you forward when you wanted to collapse."

"Be merciful."

"Forgive others."

"Reevaluate the groups you're in."

"Write paper lists for groceries again."

"Take time to be thoughtful in birthday cards."

"Take time to write your signature. Don't rush it."

"These are the things that people need to hear right now."

"They must hear them."

"Listen to Sarah."

"Listen to Sarah, Sarah Femme For Short."

"They all have a Sarah. It is the voice in their head."

"Christmas colors are important."

"People have gotten away from the traditional Christmas colors. They know it doesn't feel right. When they see the traditional green and red, it brings back memories. Christmas isn't trendy. It is the celebration of the birth of baby Jesus."

Messages

During our conversations, Sarah told me that there is a constant battle for messaging in almost everything we see daily. She said from books to songs, to billboards…everything has a message.

"Some of these messages are from Santa Claus if people would just pay attention."

She said that He is using the "artists" to send messages to everyone.

Sarah also said, "You are placed at the right place and at the right time" to see and hear the messages that are meant for you.

Looking back at this now, I do realize that the music lyrics are very powerful.

I guess I've always known this.

From Jelly Roll's "Save Me" to Beyoncé's "Halo," Celine Dion's "A New Day Has Come" and even Tracy Chapman's "Fast Car." Sarah said that music lyrics are used as a form of "communication from Him to you and from you to Him."

After Sarah told me this, I started paying more attention to the actual words in songs. The meaning of those words. What was the artist really trying to say in the lyrics? What are the real messages?

If you actually listen to the lyrics and hear them—I mean, really listen to them—you will hear there are messages throughout the lyrics for people who are struggling and need to hear those words.

Those lyrics offer hope.

She said that people weren't praying enough but that some songs and music lyrics were a form of prayer to Him.

If you listen to Aaron Lewis's/Staind song "It's Been Awhile," the majority of the song sounds as if Aaron is singing/talking to Him.

Eminem's "Not Afraid" is similar. Alanis Morissette's "Everything" sounds almost exactly like she is talking to Him.

She said that music is a gift, and it's very important to really listen to the lyrics. Honestly, Sarah's words to me about music and the significant power of lyrics have changed my life since she made the statements, and I've started to evaluate the words more definitively. I frequently find myself amazed. A very large portion of the time that a potential song is written about a love interest can usually be easily redirected from us to Him and from Him to us.

Love songs are very powerful, and it's interesting that most songs in our world are about love in some way. We have love, we look for love, we find love, we lose love, and we agonize over love. Love. Love. Love.

Toward the end of January/early February (2024), and after I started writing the book when I had moments of time to gather my thoughts and organize my Sarah notes, I'd sat down and watched the movie *The Greatest Showman*.

I'd been looking for a different movie I'd had saved on the television but decided on *The Greatest Showman* because I couldn't find the other movie after searching for it several times.

I remembered loving the soundtrack as I turned it on.

I'd been trying to take my mind off what I thought would be an enormous task in writing this book. (In actuality, though, this book only took me about a solid week to write when I had a few hours here and there.)

Seeing that movie with new eyes myself, and actually listening to the words of most of the songs, after Sarah told me about all the messaging from Him in the lyrics, I was completely amazed.

If you have not seen this movie in a while, it is worth a revisit. Take a listen to the lyrics and look at them through His eyes as if he is singing them to you or you are singing to him. The soundtrack and lyrics of every song in *The Greatest Showman* can quite literally make you a different and better person if you listen to the songs in the manner I've described above, the way Sarah explained. What is interesting about music (and books too) is that a person can listen to a song (or read a book) at different times in their life and get completely different messages and meanings from those words. As we change in our lives, the human brain sees information and meaning in various ways.

I am betting that if your mind is open and the timing is right for you, you will begin to see music in a manner that can and will be life-changing if you allow the lyrics to touch your soul and see it as a messaging tool to or from the other side.

Sarah Continued

She said, "People need to really think about what they allow into their hearts and what they allow into their minds. [Message: What you think about, you bring about.]"

Sarah also said that the choices we make every single day in who we choose to surround ourselves with are of utmost importance. (Message: Choose your friends wisely. Friends can bring you up or they can bring you down. Your choice.")

Sarah said people weren't "praying enough."

(Now I didn't pray regularly, and if I did, I'd felt I didn't have any idea what I was doing, and I wasn't praying in the correct way. I'd often choose to not pray at the dinner table or bedtime because I didn't want to sound or look stupid.)

Regarding praying, Sarah told me that it doesn't matter if you've never prayed.

"All that matters is that you do it."

She told me you do not have to be on your knees or in a special place.

"It doesn't have to be at a certain time of day."

She said that many people pray on "the toilet" although that had decreased significantly in recent years, and "toilet praying" was okay.

In fact, it's encouraged.

She laughed at one point and said, "He hears it all."

Sarah told me that there were a lot of people out there like me who were suffering from insomnia.

She said, "People need to rest. It is critical to their health and well-being."

She said, "If counting bleating sheep doesn't do it for someone who is trying to fall asleep, then picture white cotton candy–type clouds. Real clouds."

She said that white clouds help to calm the mind.

She also said, "Look at the light shining through the clouds in the daytime."

And since I'm talking about what she said about clouds, I feel this is a segue into another thing she told me.

She said, "Boof doesn't like the color white."

She encouraged me to wear white when I could.

She told me to notice the rainbows. They have significant meaning.

She went even further and said that I must write in the book that the word *love* may be the most important word we ever say *and* think as humans.

Regarding sleeping, she said, "If you're having trouble sleeping, to do this. Close your eyes. Inhale deeply. Hold your breath for two to three seconds and exhale saying the word *love* to yourself."

She said, "Do this over and over. Your mind will begin to rest."

(Of course, until I gave in and just started writing this book, that love method never worked for me. It was only after I started typing that Sarah let me sleep a little, and I found that her love method helped to calm my mind a bit.)

There was one more thing Sarah told me when it came to the word *love*.

She said the word *love* has so much power.

She urged everyone to just repeat the word "Love…love…love…" and breathe deeply if they are ever scared, nervous, anxious, stressed out, or just not feeling right.

Also regarding the "home," she said to let in light to your home whenever you can.

Open the shades or blinds and let the sunshine come through.

"Boof doesn't like sunshine. He doesn't like light."

She also said that Boof loves clutter and dark spaces."

She encouraged me to clear anything out of my home that I didn't "need" or "love."

She said, "Dog hair doesn't matter. Stop worrying about the dog hair. You aren't a hairless home, so what if you have hair on your clothes or find a piece of your dog's hair on a plate? Get over it."

Sarah was so loving in her voice as she often tried to find the words I'd understand, but she was all business at times.

She told me to start taking the time to enjoy the tasks around my home that I didn't want to do and that clearing out belongings that no longer served me would help me to enjoy the tasks (like putting away laundry in a cramped closet) I'd procrastinated in doing.

She'd say, "Make your home your personal sanctuary."

"Only allow things into your home that you need or love."

K-Love

At one point during my sleepless week(s) in January, Sarah was in my dreams, and she'd told me that I needed to clear out some things from my house. She'd said I should start with some jewelry and books and old eyeglasses.

One day, during the week, utterly exhausted and unable to sleep during the day, I made myself busy after making my bed and cleared out a bunch of jewelry that reminded me of the past, books I'd accumulated and read or would never read, and old eyeglasses that had cost me a fortune in frames.

I loaded up a box, got in the car, and drove towards a little church in my town that I know gives donated items straight to other people in town that are in need.

On the way to donate my items to the little church, I was just so fatigued from not sleeping that I felt I was almost in tears.

I thought about the past and how I'd had to hire a nice teenage girl to sleep at my house and babysit for me while I worked graveyard shifts with my promotion to lieutenant in the police department.

I thought about the people I knew and worked with who actually went to a doctor to get a "permission slip" to be exempt from working the night shift while I struggled to try to sleep during the day and work all night.

I thought about how unbelievably difficult working nights had been for me.

Why was I still holding on to this resentment? And yes, it was unfair, but you got through it, I thought.

Why was I carrying so much pain still?

On my way to the church, I was listening to a country music station.

I'd listened to this station quite a bit and rarely ever veered away from it unless someone else was in the car. The station was saved to my device and easy for me to play without much thought.

Exhausted, I started crying. I literally started crying while driving down the street.

While staring out the front window of my car with tears in my eyes, I said simply, "Jesus, I can't do this alone. I need your help."

And that was it.

The radio channel I'd been listening to change *on its own* in my car.

It literally went from the country music channel I'd been listening to, to a channel that showed up on my vehicle screen only as "K-Love."

I thought, *Am I seeing this? Is this really on my car screen right now?* I'd often named my devices with a "K" in front of the name (like K-Phone, K-Pad, etc.), but this…?

I didn't even know that radio station existed.

I'd never listened to it in my life that I'm aware of, and I saw the first initial of my own name (K) and the word "Love" in the title.

(Sarah told me that love is the most powerful word in language, right?)

The sounds of uplifting, hope-filled, inspirational music filled my car.

Words that I absolutely needed to hear in that moment filled my ears and heart.

So of course, at that moment, I do what?

Well, since you asked, I went from crying to straight-up bawling.

Not just bawling, I mean full-blown wailing—the kind of wailing that most people would feel embarrassed and uncomfortable to witness.

I continued to the church, trying to get myself together.

In my rush to get to the church at donation opening time, I'd neglected to see that I was about forty-five minutes early for my offering of donated items as the church was only open on specific days and times for donations.

I pulled into the church and saw a man walking out the side door.

I'd recognized him as a church volunteer in my other visits there throughout the year, and I asked him if I could drop off my items, knowing I was a little early.

He said, "Yes, that would be fine," and at that moment, I could not control the flood of tears that came to my eyes.

By that time, another gentleman church volunteer approached the back of my car as they both attempted to unload the items I'd brought.

Seeing this woman in tears, they of course were instantly uncomfortable.

They asked if they could help. I shook my head no.

They asked if I'd lost someone. I just shook my head no.

What could I tell these guys?

I am being stalked in my dreams by an utterly relentless angel I named Sarah who told me I had to write a book before she'd stop her visits to my dreams and just let me sleep.

"I have an angel stalker!"

Nope. I just donated my items, got in my car, heaved a couple of deep breaths in between tears, and drove away.

White Feathers

There was one last thing that occurred during my week of insomnia that I must tell you.

There were hundreds of people in Montana who witnessed this event, and I'm sure they will reflect in their own memories if they happen to read this book.

Sarah told me throughout the week that I needed to look for white feathers.

She said, any feather actually applies but the white feathers are specifically important because the white feathers are gifts from your guardian angels.

Throughout the week, she'd shown me upward of ten white feathers, and they appeared at the most needed times.

She'd told me I could not ever expect to see them.

They must be a "surprise" to me.

She'd said I would see the white feathers at the time I most needed to see them.

Toward the end of the week, barely functional with sleep deprivation, I attended a dance recital in the Valley I live in.

I'd attended dozens of dance recitals in recent years and never seen something like this.

At the end of the dance recital, a group of about six to eight teenage dancers began to act out a pillow fight in their dance.

At the end of the music, the entire stage became engulfed in white feathers from their pillow fight.

I kid you not.

I sat there, tired, amazed, and just wanting a solid nap.

"Am I seeing this right now?"

"Is Mindy McCready's song '10,000 Angels' coming to life on the stage in front of me?"

There must have been at least ten thousand white feathers floating around the dance stage at that moment.

At the end of the dance, as people with large dust brooms cleared the layer of white fluff from the floor, the owner of the studio told the audience that she hadn't known those feathers would be part of the show at all.

She went on to say they were actually a "surprise" to her.

Honeybees

(Sarah told me to tell you about the bees)

Sarah insisted I put my limited knowledge of honeybees at the end of this book. She'd said, "The bees are important."

I protested in my dreams and said adding bees at the end of a book like this would look silly, like an afterthought. I told her the bees would look out of place.

She'd simply replied, "Bees are much more than an afterthought."

At some point during the sleepless week, I remember Sarah telling me in my dreams that my honeybees were alive.

I guess she'd known I'd been worrying about them?

January 2024 was so strange, weather-wise.

We'd go from lows in the single digits at night to fifty degrees Fahrenheit in the daytime.

I'd begun to worry about our tree leaves budding too early believing it was spring and how my small apiary of honeybees was fairing through the chaotic weather.

I'd only been a beekeeper for two years at this point.

When I'd retired in 2014, I'd told my family I was curious about bees and wanted to try my hand at caring for them.

I never really consumed much in the way of honey, but bees had always been intriguing to me.

In 2016 or so, my husband bought me my first beekeeping suit and smoker.

It literally sat in a closet for almost five years until I finally decided to go for it.

After the darkness of COVID-19 left somewhat, I started to have renewed interest in raising honeybees.

I attended my first bee class Honeybees 101 and began beekeeping with my first and only hive in the spring of 2022.

I remember a lady telling me when I went to pick up my sole nuke that I should maybe buy two nukes so that I had a basis for comparison between hives.

In bee terms, a nuke is basically a small honeybee colony created from larger colonies.

My nuke had a queen that had already been introduced and accepted by the colony.

What is funny about queens and really misunderstood by most people is that they really aren't in charge of the hive and they only serve to produce fertilized and unfertilized eggs to the hive, depending on what sex of bee is needed at that time.

The colony can decide at any time that the queen isn't producing what the hive needs any longer and they will end her life.

Queens typically live between three to five years if the colony approves of her.

In retrospect, I'm not sure purchasing two nukes would have made a difference in my first year of beekeeping.

The winter of 2022–2023 was unbelievable and many livestock and human beings died because of the cold in the Northern States.

While bees are amazing and keep their hives at ninety-eight degrees by vibrating their bodies and balling up together around the queen, even in winter, my first colony of bees sadly perished that first year.

The beekeeper may have made some whopping mistakes in winterizing them too.

In the spring of 2023, I purchased two nukes and set out to give the whole beekeeping thing another try.

Immediately, I could tell that one of the nuke colonies was very slow and lethargic while the other nuke was lively and active.

I checked on the hives periodically through the late spring and early summer and found that the lethargic hive never really took hold.

I'd given them the same care that I gave to the other hive, but they still struggled.

Going into winter 2023/2024, I left almost all the honey frames in my strong hive for them to be able to make it successfully through winter, and I did the same with my lethargic hive in addition to other feed supplements to help them live.

After I had the dream of Sarah, telling me that my bees were alive, I ventured out in the snow one day to check on my two hives.

It was about fifty degrees, and the sun was shining.

I'd been so tired from the lack of sleep, but I thought the sunshine on my face, and some fresh air would help me sleep that night.

When I arrived at my two honeybee hives, I was a little shocked at first.

I immediately saw no activity coming from the lethargic hive.

Nothing had changed in the entrance from the last time I'd walked out to visit them.

The hive was still and quiet.

I looked at my active hive and saw something completely different from the lethargic hive.

I saw dead bees all over the front of the hive!

They were in the grass, on the snow, and the "front porch" (if you will) of the hive. (The front portion of the hive where their small entrance is.)

There were so many of them! Dead bees everywhere!

Now you may ask why this was exciting for me to see, so here it is.

Honeybees do so many amazing things, and the fact that they remove all the dead bees from their hive is just one of those amazing things.

I lowered myself to peer into the hive entrance.

I'd minimized the entrance at the start of winter to help keep the hive warmer and help prevent unwanted intruders from the hive.

What I saw took my breath away.

Two single female worker bees were each carrying dead bees through the entrance/exit and out onto the front porch.

They'd lift an entire dead bee body by themselves and try to push the lifeless bee body over the edge of the porch in a bee-style funeral.

I knew that the strong active hive lived, and I was very happy to see it.

I thought of Sarah in my dream, and I smiled.

As I started to walk away from my two beehives, I noticed something else that just made my day.

The snow we'd received in the first couple weeks of January was white and beautiful.

It had that "crunchy" sound to it as I walked through it in my boots.

I always joke that my life is surrounded by poop, and it basically is—cow poop, dog poop, chicken poop, turkey poop, horse poop, and now honeybee poop!

Scattered all over the top of the snow were tiny little yellow and brownish/yellow honeybee poops!

Honeybees will not poop or (defecate) in their hives.

During the coldest months, they save it all up until the temperature outside reaches about forty-five to fifty degrees Fahrenheit.

Once it's warm enough outside, the honeybees will take what's known as a cleansing flight and relieve themselves.

I was literally looking at a giant honeybee toilet in the snow, and nothing could make me happier at that moment.

My honeybees were indeed alive, just like Sarah told me in my dreams!

Only one to two months later while awaiting the publication of this book, I'd found that my lethargic beehive not only made it through the winter too, but it was looking even stronger than the other hive as the weather warmed. While I hadn't seen any activity in the month of January as I'd observed in the other hive, both hives made it!

Conclusion

At one moment during our conversations in my dreams, I was frustrated and asked Sarah, "Why must I write this book and look 'vulnerable' as you asked me to do and write a book that would open me up to so much criticism?"

She replied simply, "Well, this is the point…you know how an avocado is perfectly ripe for about fifteen minutes?"

I replied, "Yes."

Sarah, Sarah Femme for Short, then said, "Well, this is our fifteen minutes."

About the Author

Photograph by Jillian Mertz Photography

Kasey Matthews Johnson is married and the mom of two living children and one child in heaven.

She lives in the Bitterroot Valley of Montana in the United States of America.

She was born and raised in Las Vegas, Nevada. She is a former Las Vegas Metropolitan Police Department police lieutenant.

She has two amazing dogs, and she and her husband raise a rare breed of furry-hardy cattle called Galloway.

Kasey has two beautiful horses Peaches and Ella, about a dozen chickens, and she tends to a small apiary of honeybees.

While raised a city girl, Kasey now loves the freedom and serenity of living in mountain country.

She is truly blessed.

Kasey didn't start this particular book willingly, but after all is said and done, she wants every reader to know "Everybody Talks to God" (Aaron Lewis).

www.ingramcontent.com/pod-product-compliance
Lightning Source LLC
Chambersburg PA
CBHW022020150726
47990CB00002B/737